Wings in the Wind

GREAT HORNED OWL

Wings in the Wind

ANNE MERRILL

Illustrations by H. T. Trevanna

THE RYERSON 18 29 PRESS - TORONTO

Published, 1954

PRINTED AND BOUND IN CANADA
BY THE RYERSON PRESS, TORONTO

TO HELEN

O magic music of the Spring,—
Across the morning's breezy meads
I hear the south wind in the reeds,
I hear the golden bluebirds sing. . . .

I see the grasses shine with dew,
The cornflowers gleaming in the grain,
And oh! the bluebirds sing—and you?
We fare together once again.

From "Bluebirds"
by Helen Merrill Egerton

Foreword

In April, 1943, Wings in the Wind started as a weekly column in *The Globe and Mail*. There was no announcement to readers, no build-up, no promotion. The feature was tossed into the cold columns of type and left to sink or soar: and how well the wings have fared in the wind ever since!

My wife and I are old friends of Anne Merrill. We had long known her enthusiasm for birds, which started when as a child she rambled 'round the shores of Prince Edward, with her father, the county judge. But, as an editor, I had thought that a weekly feature would be justified only in that brief period each year when Canadians are so conscious that winter is suddenly over and the birds are back.

Anne was asked to write her feature for a month. It has run ever since—without any further discussion about how long it would run. But it was not Anne Merrill's great knowledge of birds—wide though it is—which made her feature a must in a crowded Saturday paper. It was Anne herself. No person can week after week, year after year, write a column about anything without letting readers know what kind of person she is. And Anne is always interesting. She likes people better than possessions. Never in her long writing career in Eastern and Western Canada and in England has she been inhibited in her expressions by economic fears or any other type of fear. Her freedom in writing what she felt has carried her column, often, far beyond the wings she started to write about.

In the last fifteen months my work has taken me to all the North Atlantic Treaty countries between Norway and Turkey. And watching the birds of Europe I have often thought about the courageous woman who taught me the little I know about the birds of Canada.

In life there are always new satisfactions. To have taken part in launching a column, which now appears in lasting book form, gives a feeling of real accomplishment.

R. A. FARQUHARSON.

Paris, France,
February 2, 1954.

viii

For Those Who Care

ONE EVENING A group of passers-by had paused on a very busy Toronto street to listen to a robin singing from the top of a telephone pole. I joined them. Was it really a robin with this song, so different—so magical?

But it was June, when the robin's song has a new tone as he sings his enchanted notes at dusk for those who care to listen.

The next day in our own street stood a big man with a small child on his shoulder, pointing out another robin piping his June roundelay from his perch in a maple tree. The look of rapture on the child's face brought a flash of memory of my own childhood in Picton. One morning my father, who greatly loved birds, carried me into the garden to see a small yellow bird on her nest, hidden among the tiny golden bell flowers of the fragrant currant bush. Father told me it was a yellow warbler. I had had my first lesson in bird identification.

As I watched my neighbour holding up his young grandson so that he could see the singing bird, I thought what a nice man he was. How thankful that child would be to the one who kindled in him a love of birds. And how very fortunate!

My excuse for this book lies in the hope, that every man who is able will hold a child up to a singing tree helping him to enter a realm of magic that could last a lifetime.

If that child be a boy may he be taught not to destroy, but to love and protect the birds so that our woods may be filled with song.

ANNE MERRILL

Toronto, May 17, 1954

Contents

1. Heralds of Spring

Robins, Horned Larks, Plovers, Crows,
Flickers, Bluebirds, Hermit Thrushes,
Sapsuckers, Phoebes

To you in Canada who care to look and to listen, there comes a season of enchantment when the big migration is on—that ever-recurring miracle of the spring. Myriads of birds, battling the prevailing winds to get here from the South, are making safe landings—the robins in our trees, meadowlarks on the open ground in country places, and the red-winged blackbird that settles among the reeds of old-gold marshes where his kind love to build.

Flocks of this handsome herald, known also as "soldier bird" because of his red epaulets, arrive at the mouth of the river and on the marsh, and any day you may hear his shrill call, at intervals, "Oka-ree! Oka-ree! Oka-ree!"

Spring is a good time—if you are not already a bird observer—to become one. Little equipment is needed to start, save enthusiasm. Given good eyes, you won't even need field-glasses, and good ears are a help, if on the alert.

Bird identifying is a lot like aircraft recognition. You note the size and silhouette of the bird and any peculiar markings.

1

ROBIN

Does it dangle its legs out behind in flight, rudder-like, as do the herons and bitterns; or does it keep them respectably tucked under until it comes to earth? Does it swoop and glide, or fly straight ahead stretching its neck forward like the wild goose or the wild swan? Does it make any sound? Is it one of the birds that sing "on the wing," or is it silent as a glider?

If you go out to some quiet place, and listen, any April evening you are likely to hear geese honking overhead. Most of the bird flights are said to take place in the night hours. One April night in Quebec, I listened for an hour to hundreds of pipings and honkings of birds in migration.

The bird migrant's first move on arrival here from the long flight—after he gets his breath and has· a bite to eat—is to stake out his claim to a building site. Males come first and assume the duties of seizing separate territory, and defending it until a party of winged ladies land within earshot a few days later, to be picked and chosen.

Watch any lawn or country woodlot in the spring. You're pretty certain to see something like this: Two cock-robins run jerkily along the turf together, eyeing each other sharply. One runs two or three feet, then the other spurts ahead, and so on, until in a flash they fly at one another, claw to claw, and test each other's mettle. The one that proves he's the best bird becomes cock of the walk—the other retreating with, or without, dignity. Sometimes both lose. One April in a friend's garden in Oakville I came on two dead robins lying on the ground, face to face, their claws hopelessly tangled.

If you wake at six o'clock and can see etched branches against a powder-blue sky, it's time to listen. You will hear a winning robin sing lustily. He calls "Hur-ee! Hur-ee! Hur-ee!" with variations, and is likely to keep it up every morning— and evening—until a lady bird comes along who likes him well enough to stay and help gather sticks and mud to build their bungalow in a tree-crotch or under some friendly eave, and set about rearing a family of little robins. And there is no lovelier bird than the robin—a wild bird at our very door— and one we may take too much for granted.

Who said "There are no birds in last year's nests?" For three successive seasons, a robin and his mate have returned to the same corn-crib on an Ontario farm, to add another nest to the structure. In the two lower berths the mud that forms part of every robin's nest has dried out, but it shows dark in the top storey. This roof garden is the nest; inside is a small bowl of mud that was

3

shaped, while plastic, by the breast of the mother bird, then wound about with grasses, leaves and weeds. Robins take mud where they find it, and may even plaster their shacks from flower-pots that have been placed out in the rain to soak. People playing hostess to birds sometimes put a pan of soft mud beside the bird bath—a chore not necessary if one has a muddy garden—to divert their energies from precious pots. Some fussy robins hang bits of string from their nests to keep up with the Jones's next door.

You will have noticed while watering your lawn that a companionable robin is likely to alight on the ground and pursue the sprinkler, pausing every few agitated steps to stop, look and listen (or whatever the bird does) for a nice, juicy earthworm.

How this bird locates a worm provides a theme for perennial argument. When the bird tilts its head, is it listening for a wriggle in the ground? Or just watching for a worm to pop out of its hole, or, as J. K. Munro suggests, do they feel, through some sensitiveness of the feet, the minute disturbance of the earth, or sod, caused by a worm's mode of locomotion? It might be a combination of these things.

I was interested to find in an article by Dale Carnegie on "How to Make Friends with Birds, and Get More Fun Out of Life," this incidental bit:

My first twenty years were spent on a Missouri farm— a paradise for birds. I remember the birds following after my father as he plowed the land, snatching at the worms the blade dug up. . . . And I remember the robin's sensitive feet feeling for a worm deep in the earth.

4

Dale Carnegie should be admitted a good seconder of J. K. Munro's theory that the robin "feels" the rising of the earthworm. But, on the other hand, Dr. Ernst Mayr, curator of the Whitney-Rothschild collections in New York museum, offers his opinion as to why a robin cocks its head while awaiting the invertebrate, stating that the bird is actually engaged in watching the earth move, and in this way locates its quarry.

When hunting worms on your lawn robins will be observed to keep carefully out of one another's way. This may be merely self-preservation, but psychologists call the behaviour "spacing."

The talk of the town one snow-clad week in Toronto was a white robin.

A lady bird, she mated with a brown robin and helped to bring up brown babies. I remember watching the white lady as she arrived, on wings, with food in her beak. How she would dart at her mate and drive him away (whenever he attempted to feed them), as much as to say: "You beat it! They are my babies."

Do not be disappointed if you do not see a white robin, for there is said to be only one albino of a species in a million.

Writing one day from Lakeland, Florida, to the Picton *Gazette*, a Prince Edward County man told of having encountered thousands of robins on their way north to Canada. Every tree in that southern town was full, as well as the sidewalks and the yards. He mentioned the camphor tree, with its small black fruit (like our wild chokecherries), on which the robins were feeding before flying off on the next lap of their long journey. Birds that are ground-feeders, such as robins, travel at night and come down to earth every morning for breakfast.

All the robins do not settle in southern Canada by any means. Hundreds go nesting as far north as the tree limits of Labrador. In recent years they have been introduced into the Old Country. I wonder how the little English robin likes the intrusion.

After nesting is over (and many pairs raise two and sometimes three broods in a season) they go off on short range flights, possibly to give their young some practice in flying, to prepare them for their eventual long journey south.

But before going away (and robins are among the last to leave) families almost invariably return to their territories in the fall, to look around the place where they spent such happy, and often anxious, days earlier in the year.

Among the earliest birds to greet the spring, vocally, in Ontario, are the horned or shore larks who like to trot around ankle-deep in the melting March snow. My sister Helen recalls spring days in Picton and the arrival of the larks there, when small flocks would come into town and feed with the sparrows in the road.

But her happiest memories of these birds were of their singing on the wing as they flew up and up into the blue and they were the inspiration for her poem, "A Hill Song," part of which reads:

6

And joy it is, the shore lark's cry—
Full well I know he walketh by;
A sudden winnow of grey wings,
And in the light he soars and sings.
And pausing in his heavenward flight,
A heart-beat, on from height to height,
He trails his silver strains of song
By paths I may not follow long.

A trifle larger than the bluebird, the lark's colouring and peculiar markings suggest the little killdeer, or semipalmated plover. He lowers his warlike tufts when he runs, and he has a long hind claw—a lark characteristic.

The only time I ever saw a lark's nest was out on the Oakville golf links where a pair raised a family in a hole on the putting green meant to receive a golf ball. It was before the open season (for golf) and the larks had just walked in and taken possession. Early players sentimentally skipped that hole (I was told) until the baby larks were able to trot off on their own little feet. The parent bird did not budge from its protective duties until our party were so near we could count four open beaks indicating an urge for food.

The longest non-stop flight I have found recorded of a land bird is 2,500 miles. This feat is credited to the golden plover that winters in the treeless pampas of the Argentine and later, in flocks of thousands, fans out all over the map, taking in the Hawaiian Islands, Alaska, and eventually Nova Scotia, in its sweep.

Is this any more incredible than the drift of the Erebus moth or the monarch butterfly, frail beauties that come in clouds all the way from South America on the wings of the wind currents?

The golden plover is related to the killdeer, whose plaintive call rises from snow-patched fields on misty mornings. He cries "Kill-deer, Kill-deer!" But he doesn't mean a thing! The plovers are known here as shorebirds, or waders, as is their cousin, the snipe; and reedy lagoons and sandy beaches seem to come alive with their stilted manoeuvres.

The killdeer is a true plover, and though listed as a shore bird, I have never yet seen one on any beach. Seems to like fields—preferably where brown earth has been turned by the plow, providing a rich feast of weevils, leather jackets and click beetles.

Was it the courting dance of the killdeer, I once watched?

The whole performance was curious and a bit comical. Intricate, too, and executed with perfect precision in spite of an accelerating tempo like the dizzying steps of a ballet finale.

I have never seen birds run so fast as the two killdeer on that late afternoon in March when I stopped to watch their amazing ballet in a playing field across the road.

At first there was only one bird in view, which I mistook for a shore lark because of the time, the place and the bird's colours. But turning on my field glasses I saw it was a killdeer plover, bobbing tiredly as if from a long migration flight.

Presently two other killdeer appeared, circling

8

overhead uttering shrill cries and coming down to land, one on either side of the grounded bird.

Leaving the tired killdeer where it stood, the two fresh arrivals from the sky started the ballet and the fun began.

Their feet flew, even though the wings were furled. They sped side by side, in close formation like twin jets. And after twenty or thirty steps the lead killdeer would stop short, and the other bird do the same. Then the first would run again, and again stop, while number two checked its own speed in a split second.

This went on and on in precise repetition, while the pair covered an incredible extent of territory from one end of the field to the other. And I had to keep my glasses at the alert so as not to miss a single measure of that extraordinary dance.

A variation was introduced into the pattern when the birds would suddenly about-turn, then run as fast in an opposite direction, their steps synchronizing like trained dancers. The second one always obeyed automatically the lead's signal to stop, go, or turn.

Once the two birds flew up a few inches above the ground and made excited leaps toward each other like fighting robins. But it was mostly bluff. The storm subsided as quickly as it had arisen, and the pair resumed their funny foot-work.

While their wings were spread, a rich, tawny orange colour flamed, and you saw killdeer in their full beauty of plumage and contour.

The most memorable sight was whenever the running birds turned to face my lookout post, and

LITTLE KILLDEER

the third killdeer came to life sufficiently to join the two in a short run. . . . Then the three identical fronts made a striking picture with their double black necklets strung around the creamy throats, the jet bands as dazzling as zebra stripes.

For forty minutes I stood and watched that dance of the killdeer, until dusk settled down, veiling their movements. And I shall never know how much longer they went on running, or when they grew tired and left the playing field for the night.

This bird is over ten inches long. But there is a smaller kind—only seven inches—which looks very much like the bird pictured here, though without the extra neckband. Books give it the unwieldy name of "semipalmated plover." When no scientists are listening in, I call it "Little Killdeer." It has a white breast and its wings are the colour of wet sand.

I saw a pair of them on the inner beach at Hanlan's Point, feeding with a flock of smaller beach-birds, the spotted sandpipers. I tried whistling and, to my surprise, one little killdeer stopped —answered the call, and made a polite bow. My

10

imitation, though synthetic, worked, and the bird called and made its funny bow, after each attempt, evidently curious to know where the queer sound came from!

W. H. Hudson—criticized by scientists, but a great popularizer of bird lore—liked the upland plover best of all the shore birds. Its cry thrilled him "above all sounds on earth," he once said. And when riding over the pampas of the Argentine, where he spent a happy boyhood, the voice of this bird, "mellowed and made beautiful by distance and the profound silence of a moonlit world," never ceased to pluck at his heartstrings.

The mystery of its migration staggered him: this frail lovely creature, "travelling in the sky alone, day and night, crying aloud at intervals as if moved by some powerful emotion, beating the air with its wings, its beak pointing like the needle of a compass to the north, flying, speeding, on its 7,000 mile flight to its nesting home in another hemisphere," its destination our Arctic.

The upland plover, in size and form somewhat like a greater yellowlegs, deserted the once familiar wading places for high and dry land. But scientists still call it a "true sandpiper."

White and grey with brown and yellow accents on upper plumage, the upland plover, when full grown, is slender with long tail and swallow-like wings. Hudson noted its pretty habit of lifting the wings straight up, in a pose suggesting "the artist's conventional figure of an angel."

A photographer once found a wingless little plover in a new-mown field, with no place to hide from potential enemies—not even the camera, he whimsically added. Its defences had been cut away by a merciless mowing machine. . . . The anxious mother bird wheeled overhead emitting querulous cries. Then after the picture session was over, she settled gracefully to the ground beside her long-legged baby and rested a moment with uplifted wings in the angelic pose recorded by Hudson.

A sad note has been sounded by many writers, including Hudson, deploring the "incalculable destruction" to bird life. Hudson cited the upland plover as "on the list of next candidates for extinction." It is protected by law on this continent, I understand. But enforcing the law—there's the rub! . . . And ironically (remembering how Hudson felt about the plover) it has no protection on the pampas where the remaining and sorely depleted flocks pass the winter.

When you watch the first strong flight of early crows as they beat their big black wings rhythmically across the pale March sky, it is a stirring sight. And when they accompany the rhythm with their spring song: "Caw! . . . caw! . . . caw!" all your old prejudice against these bold, bad birds vanishes, at least for the time—and if you're not a corn planter!

In husky major-thirds, their voice interprets spring to you better than Mendelssohn. It has the feel of stormy sunrise, ragged clouds and wild wind. The advance guard fills you with a new respect. The crows are going places. They seem to know what they want and mean to get it. They

12

may be heading for familiar fields where young tender shoots are creeping upward, under the surface of the brown earth. They know.

The farmer knows, too. And out may come the scarecrow from his toolshed. My county of Prince Edward was a famous place for this weird contraption. Driving along any country road there, we saw scarecrows. In fantastic forms they would dangle from slanting poles in almost every field, until their shape grew so familiar to the wily crow that he was occasionally observed to use one for a foot rest!

If you want a spirited argument on your hands—either at a debating club or in a newspaper—just proclaim that the crow should (or should not) be exterminated. The controversy is likely to go on until the referee, or the editor, cries "Enough!"

The bird has been called a black rascal, a pirate, a gangster, and a rarin' devil because he sometimes eats the eggs and young of other birds, including game birds.

Well—how clear is our (human) conscience when we broil squabs for our own delight—not just to provide sustenance for young families, as is the crow's excuse. Have we ever indulged in baby quail on toast, or thrown live lobsters into a boiling pot to make them more tasty? It might be well to think on these things before condemning the crow.

Some farmers may mutter imprecations. Others are out to welcome them, knowing their value and recalling perhaps what a great conservationist (the late C. Gordon Hewitt of Ottawa) once said, that

"Crows are to no small extent friends of the farmer, since they consume immense quantities of white grubs—one of our worst agricultural pests."

And as you look up at that big jet-black silhouette against the brilliant blue of the sky and watch those wide scissor-cut wings swiftly flapping, as the crow races with the scudding white clouds torn to tatters by the winds of March, you will feel a queer surge of spring in your heart when you hear his noisy challenge to the world.

Coming down to earth, the crow is readily tamed and makes an interesting pet. One writer says it has a happier knack of learning "man-like tricks" than any other bird. My father once tamed two crows at our old home in Picton. He called them Peter and Patter. They would follow him down to the shore, where he kept his sailboats, pick up his tools—when he wasn't looking—and fly off with them. Or they would take clothespins off the line; and steal our bright toys.

Henry Ward Beecher is credited with saying that if men were clad in feathers few of them would be smart enough to enter the crow class.

Like its cousin, the magpie, the crow has a sense of humour, a very good thing in both bird and man.

English people often ask if we have magpies in Canada. The answer is yes. They are found west of the Great Lakes, north to middle Yukon, and in Southern British Columbia, except the coast district. Evidently, magpies are not fond of salt water. They range the prairie country, too, where

14

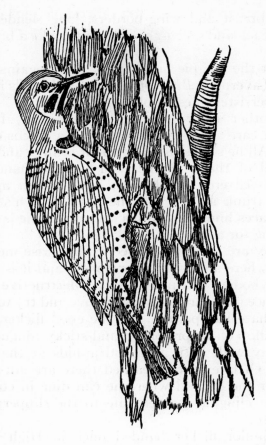

FLICKER

they do scavenger duty, cleaning up the scraps after stock is butchered.

Grouped in bird books with the crow, magpies are equally prankish and would make good entertainers at a party. They are more graceful in flight than the crow, and very handsome. The flashing white breast and wing-borders, long slender tail, black back and green-glossed head, make a brilliant show.

But the magpie has a black mark against it in P. A. Taverner's *Birds of Canada*. He calls it "the most persistent nest robber in the world."

Another early arrival is the flicker, for he doesn't care a rap whether there is a crocus out or not. All he seems to think about is ants, and trees are full of them. When you see this handsome sequin-spattered woodpecker with his ear against a tree trunk as he grips the bark with his claws and braces himself with his spiked tail, he is likely listening for ants.

Why are the ants in trees? Birdwise men say that's where ants search for honey, and it is found in the bodies of aphids—those destructive little plant-lice that garden folk who love and try to grow roses, hate like poison. So the good flicker, with one wallop of his prolonged and sticky tongue, can do away with both ants and aphids at the same time. Of late he has learned there are ant-heaps all over the ground where he can dine in comfort without clinging for dear life to the slippery side of a tree.

A junior flicker banded once in High Park, Toronto, was reported months later, hammering for ants in a forest in South America. One of its names is the yellow hammer.

The flicker is called by some sixty different names—apart from the ones the ants call him—which explains why the scientists use Latin names for birds—to make identification easy.

Flickers resemble robins in their taste for weather—happiest when rain is in the air. Then they call and call, and I am never quite sure if they are crying for more rain, or sending out a signal (like the rainbow) that rain is over for the present.

One day I noticed a flicker in full voice, with no apparent relation to the weather. He found a ready-made hole, well up in a big willow tree near the wildfowl pond, and would dive down inside the hole and disappear, then in a few seconds show himself again, stick his head (and neck) out of the opening, and blow his shrill horn in an incessant series of toots.

He would sound off, turn his head from side to side, looking or listening—wait a second—then start all over again, darting in and out of the hole as if trying it for size and comfort.

An answering bugle call came from a distance (prospective mate presumably) and Mr. Flicker seemed to be telling her, over the airwaves, that here was a first-rate site for a nest. . . . She'd better hurry along if she wanted to share his bungalow—or else.

He might go hunting elsewhere for a more responsive mate.

The strategy worked. Presently the other flicker arrived at the willow and there followed a ceremonial bowing of the two woodpeckers, when I had to leave the scene to catch the ferry back to town. But no doubt everything was settled satisfactorily before any other pair of birds could contest their rights to that nesting site.

The flicker holes up in stumps or dead trees,

17

and many go modern by tunnelling in telegraph poles along country roads. Their cave may be from one to two feet deep, chiselled—a chip at a time, which they toss to the ground, though a few are left at the bottom of nest cavity for bedding.

Usually five to nine glossy white eggs are laid. Though once when a nest was persistently robbed, it is on record that Mrs. Flicker continued to make replacements in the clutch, up to seventy-one eggs in seventy-three days.

They eat wood-boring ants, and many grubs. When young flickers grow big and strong enough, they scramble up to the tunnel mouth and await grubs. The late Henry F. Pullen, a West Coast observer, suggested that the word "grub" (as used in logging camps, for food) could have come from this woodpecker habit.

It is most unusual for flickers to winter here. It is the one member of the woodpecker family that seems to prefer warmer climes. But birds have done unusual things; one winter a Toronto reader of *Wings in the Wind* was surprised to see a flicker on an evergreen tree outside the kitchen window, eating the fat that had been spread on the tree for birds. Then it flew to the feeding-box, where it spent half an hour eating from a tray of bread crumbs, pieces of fat and other scraps.

And so, long before the leaves unfurl, the air is bright with wings, obstinate April having failed to discourage them. And the lovely, gentle blue-birds are already in the orchards and singing atop country fence posts. What brings these flocks so

18

early when there seems nothing visible to attract them? They've come to seize their territorial rights, of course, each male bird taking possession of an extent of land sufficient to fill food requirements for himself and family later, when millions of insects become unfrozen and come out for the sole purpose of being eaten!

Now it is a hermit thrush, that hardy member of the thrush family that comes north long before its relatives. It has a whitish breast, studded at the throat with brown dots, dark brown eyes with light eye-rims, and its head, wings and back are an even olive-beige. The flesh-tinted legs are slender. The mark of identification is the tail which has a tawny touch.

The hermit's song, when in the wildwood, is something to rave about — it is said to resemble that tempestuous and wild movement that opens the finale of Beethoven's Moonlight Sonata—but I've never heard it give, within the city limits, more than the curved callnote, "Whee-you!"

On a tree-flanked height overlooking one of the marshes I saw my first sapsucker of the season. All the authorities agree that the sapsucker is a bad bird—the one injurious member of the woodpecker family. But like many another villain in the play, you must admit he's a good-looking rascal!

Especially, if you happen to catch him gallivanting with the spring sun glinting on his jaunty red velvet crest, and on the matching red throatpiece that fluffed out prettily every time he uttered his rather musical whine. In contrast to this flaring headlight, the sapsucker's coat and breast-plate had a quiet effect, like pale gold filtered through black lace.

The sapsucker is definitely a migrant, and this was the first of his kind to visit us that year. His bright eye didn't miss a trick as he clawed his jerky way among the tasselled twigs of a young elm, stopping every step or two to poke his long bill into the French knots wherein he found sweets to his liking or maybe insect meat.

The sapsucker's fondness for the sweet inner layer (called cambium) beneath the bark of trees leads it to puncture the tree full of holes. It also likes to stay and sip copiously, with its brush-like tongue, of the sap which exudes—hence the bird's name.

Later, when the juices surge up in the trees, the sapsucker really gets busy with its iron punch, drilling evenly-spaced holes, like double-sixes, from which it drinks the sap.

In a Sherbrooke cemetery a few years ago I observed a curious instance of the way some other birds take advantage of the pecker's skill in carpentry. . . . And by the way it was then I first discovered what a special sanctuary for birds a cemetery could be. . . . No boys with BB guns, no collectors, no cats!

No sooner had a sapsucker finished its supper (or sipper) at the table of holes it had punched in the trunk of a tall birch, than an alert humming-bird buzzed over to the tree and alighted at one of the holes where it clung in exactly the same manner as any woodpecker with its tiny, stubby tail comically braced against the bark.

The hummingbird probed the hole as it would a trumpet flower, and darted its cloven tongue out of its long beak (though I could not see this part of the performance) to glean any of the sweet sap the woodpecker might have left.

A plaintive note in the spring symphony is the gentle cry of the phoebe.

To distinguish the phoebe quickly from other flycatchers, watch the tail—a good field mark. If the bird wags it sideways, like a young puppy (not up and down like a pump-handle) the correct guess is phoebe. Olive grey above and creamy below, it is a trifle larger than the wood pewee and with darker head. It has no light wing-bars like the pewee.

The phoebe's other name is "bridge pewee," owing to its favourite nesting site on projections, under bridges, and near water, where it can get mud and moss for its nest. Because the usual four or five young phoebes do not leave home until fully armed for flight, few meet disaster by tumbling overboard. The eggs are white, and in a few instances have brown spots.

Lady Phoebe herself builds the house. First she plasters a mud foundation, mixed with moss, where moss is available. It is funny to see her flying from the shore—her mouth so full of building material, it sticks out at either side, like green whiskers. The inner cup is lined with fine grass

21

and feathers and (where horses are still in vogue) a few strands of horsehair are woven in.

Though her mate does not help in the construction of the nest, he goes with her on these trips for "lumber," and cheers her morale by constantly calling, "Phee . . . bee! . . . Phee . . . bee!" And he helps to fly out and catch dancing gnats and other good "eats," when the fledglings arrive.

You do not have to go further afield than your own back yard to see marvellous birds in their gay spring plumage. Just turn and look out of your own window.

2. The Flower Birds

Warblers, Scarlet Tanagers, Orioles,
Bobolinks, Redstarts, Catbirds, Vireos,
Hummingbirds, Cuckoos

THROUGH THE YEARS I have learned to associate the arrival of certain birds with the blossoming of particular flowers or budding trees. Fields full of yellow dandelions in the country bring the tinkling bobolink. When the sticky buds of the horse chestnut tree unfold, look for the scarlet tanager. And with the apple blossoms, the gaily liveried oriole comes weaving from perch to perch among the flowers, while the mosquito plane of the bird fleet (the hummingbird) awaits the signal of the honeysuckle and the trumpet flower before boarding one of the feathered aircraft carriers—the wild swan or maybe a Canada goose, to transport him north.

When trees are bursting into full leaf, watch for the incoming waves of warblers sparkling like coloured jewels as each wave breaks over the tree tops, and tinkling like tiny bells when the ballets disperse into individual dances and each feathery sprite finds a leafy perch on which to stand and rejoice in safety after his hazardous flight.

Warblers are among the birds that migrate

HOODED WARBLER

by night and are very vulnerable, in danger of being drawn from their course like moths, by powerful lights. Lighthouses were the chief source of bird tragedies formerly. Now it seems that strong lights in any high tower exert an equal fascination for night-flying birds.

The wood warblers of the world are of a very large and fascinating variety. Their family tree has branches that wave over five continents. Some are found in the enchanted isles of the Southwest Pacific; they begin to arrive early in May—at first singly, then in straggling bands; and then the woods are aglitter with a gay confusion of colour, contour and song. After a few days here to rest and feed, many warblers will fly away to the northern spruce woods to nest. Some, like the yellow warbler, stay in Southern Canada. Yellow warblers build intricate nests shaped like beautiful cradles woven of fine grass, quilted and lined with softest plant-down and securely tied to upright posts in the crotch of small trees.

The yellow warbler is one of the few birds clever enough to outwit the cowbird, who has the strange habit of laying its unwanted eggs in other birds' nests. I was sent once a four-decker nest and on each of the three lower floors, showing through woven dried grasses, was a cowbird's egg, neatly roofed over by a warbler.

The Canada warbler is sometimes called "Canada Necklace," because of the heavy jet fringe strung across its bright yellow dickie. Matching the vest is a pair of gold eye-rims, giving a goggled effect.

It likes to nest on or near the ground in some cool, moist woods carpeted with moss. Its hide-out is woven of rootlets, grass and shreds of bark. Not a climber, it forages mainly in low branches.

Early writers called this bird Canada fly-catcher because of its dexterity in snapping up flies on the wing.

When the lovely magnolia tree is in bloom along our avenue, by a happy scientific coincidence, the magnolia warblers are here.

They flash into view and perch for a precious minute, long enough to permit an inventory. . . . Magnolia warbler, done in black, white and yellow . . . White wing-patches glinting on blue-black wings . . . Black arrow across each eye and a wide black band to square off the decorative tail.

But the real beauty of the bird is in its butter-cup vest, laced down the front with jagged black stripes, like the Canada warbler's necklace, only longer. Look for him among willows, beside the water, spreading his pretty wings and conspicuous tail after the showy manner of a redstart.

This bird was once called black-and-yellow

warbler, but as the same colours were sported by the Canada warbler, prairie warbler and Cape May warbler, it was decided to allay confusion by changing its name to Magnolia. The nest is interesting—the outside framework made of fine twigs, sometimes (it is said) held together by knots of spider's silk. Inside is a cup woven of finer leaf-stems, lined with fluff. Its summer tenant winters from Southern Mexico to Panama, and on occasions, in Puerto Rico and Cuba.

The bird sensation of the spring of 1946 was the arrival in Ontario of a number of hooded warblers— nobody knows how many—a southern bird with only a few records of its ever having appeared so far north before, and a month ahead of any previously recorded visit. Stuart Thompson saw one here in 1907, and not more than fifteen have been observed in this region in a hundred years, states Dr. R. M. Saunders, editor Toronto Field Naturalists' *Newsletter*.

First report to reach me came from Arthur W. Preston, Port Dover, who had watched the bird on Sunday, April 6th—an adult male hooded warbler —having been called to see the rarity by a neighbour lad, William Parkinson Jr. In his letter, Mr. Preston asked what brought this bird up here by such an early date. "Did it get blown in on some recent storm?" he wondered. His guess was right. It came on the wings of the wind!

Mr. Preston's theory was confirmed by Dr. Saunders. Citing meteorological information on storms of that time, he said: "It would seem that the storm caught up a group of migrating hooded warblers and other small birds, and whisked them far up into this inhospitable spring."

This warbler winters from Vera Cruz to Panama, and while it breeds chiefly in the Louisiana to Florida region, it has been found nesting as far north as the southern fringe of Michigan. Its appearance in Ontario has always come as a surprise—and in April, a pleasant shock!

The bird to watch for—if you would see this *rara avis*—is five inches long. The male has a jet black hood, encircling head and neck like a visor; a bright yellow face, forehead and breast, and an olive back. Has a forked tail. Its song is not unlike, in timbre, the northern yellow throat, but with different accent. It has been set down by one listener as "Weeta . . weeteo . . weeta . . weeteo," falling in a musical cadence at end of phrase.

The black-throated blue warbler is a dapper little fellow with blue back and wings, has a large white patch on midwing, and a white breast. A velvet-black front runs up to the sharp little beak and under the eye, then down in curved margin along shoulder of wing. When the bird fans its short, square tail, white bands flash.

All the enchanting birds coming north at this time of year stay here such a tantalizingly short while, that we ought to try and get out to see (and identify) as many as possible before they fly away to the northern evergreen woods.

Especially those wild little warblers, so lovely yet maddeningly elusive. . . . Look for small dappled birds with restless wings and lisping notes . . . a blackburnian in the birches; a black-and-white, creeping up the trunk of a pine; a chestnut-sided in the shrubbery; a little black-throated blue warbler that hops quietly about and looks like a tiny blue jay.

Then there is the mourning warbler, though far from sad, whose name came from fancied crepe-like marks on its throat. It ranges across Canada to the Alberta foothills.

Indeed it would take a lifetime to learn to identify all the varieties. For James Bond, writing of warblers in the *Audubon Magazine*, mentions 115 species, fifty-four of which nest on this continent. The Old World warblers are dull in colour but "superlative singers," he remarks, while ours are gaily plumed but poor vocalists.

Make the blossoming trees your bird guide and you will see a tanager, in flaming colour like flower-cups of the scarlet runner, exploring white clusters on the wild cherry tree—its small jet wing the only foil for so much red.

Watch, if you can, that magnet for feathers—an oriental quince tree covered with very pink and honied flowers.

To this tree come hummingbirds, orioles, towhees and catbirds. Orioles dip into each cup as their bodies sway the slim branches. We know about the hummingbirds, but can any one tell if the orioles are sipping honey or raindrops from the pink cups, or (as I've often wondered) do they sniff the fragrance? If not, what then are a bird's nostrils for?

Orioles are strangely drawn to the willow tree. Chinese artists have noted this, and you will frequently find the bird and the tree combined in a picture. Rated as a "feminine" tree in China, dancers in long sleeves and flowing robes try to simulate the movement of willow branches as they sway and bow in the wind—says Lin Yutang.

Conceded to be the most beautifully constructed nest in the bird world, an oriole's nest is a marvel of bird architecture, woven of fine plant-fibre and string, and hitched securely to connecting tips of one of the highest willow or elm branches to be found in the pair's selected territory. It is said that the Baltimore oriole got his name because he wears the black and orange family colours of Lord Baltimore. He is also called the golden robin.

"Do orioles occupy the same nest year after year?" I asked an authority on construction. No, he said, though the birds might use bits of the old material—pull last year's nest apart and weave

29

some of it into shape with fresh fibres to give it that new look.

Discussions occur perennially among naturalists as to the kind of string preferred by orioles. Experts are found on both sides, some declaring that these bright birds naturally select strands of gay-coloured wool. Others say, just as firmly, that pale pastels are preferred—common white string, or weather-stained bits resembling root fibres which fit into their scheme of camouflage.

But whichever kind of string we may helpfully decide to put out where orioles can find it, we should be sure to cut it into short pieces, not more than six inches in length. For it is on record that many bird tragedies have resulted from legs becoming hopelessly entangled in long strings.

There is also a perennial argument among bird observers as to whether the lady alone constructs their marvellous nest. Some say Lord B. leaves her to do all the work. Though none have disputed the fact that—when the family arrives—he brings home the ants!

Which reminds me to pass on a hint offered by Wallace Havelock Robb of Abbey Dawn, near Kingston, Ontario:

I suggest that you tip off your readers to imitate the oriole when he sings. . . . His song is varied and captivating. But it is clearcut, in easily imitated phrases. If he considers the imitation good enough to be considered competition, or so bad that it enrages him, the result may be thrilling.

I have had one singing back at me until so annoyed that he came down from the tree top to within five feet of me, fussing and scolding and then singing his full song right in my face!

When the sun's magnetic fingers begin to play upon the keys of spring, drawing up dandelions out of the lush grass like a myriad of yellow tufts on a green satin counterpane, it's time to look—and listen—for the bobolink. He likes to choose his scenery.

It is then he comes a-courting, in motley attire, with black dignity in front, and harlequin rear—a fashion in reverse. The back of his tailed coat is criss-crossed in white and there's a fringe of daisy petals showing where his wing-sleeves fold. But the key-note is that odd yellow patch low at the back of his head, as though his cap had slid off when he was flying. Looks like a faded, pressed dandelion, kept for sentiment rather than beauty.

When courting, the bobolink rises a few feet above his quiet brown mate, in hiding among the dandelions, and serenades her, on the wing—his song like the tinkling of tiny glass balls sprinkled over a floor of gold. The other June, I watched a fleet of five romantic males, poised overhead on fluttering wings, and all singing at once in enchanting waves of sound.

What a pity that this happy songster—paying high dividends while here, with its lovely music, its beauty (and enormous appetite for grasshoppers)—becomes a hunted menace in the autumn when it reaches the rich ricefields of South Carolina, where it is said to be slaughtered in thousands.

These handsome and tinkling songsters have not always been as popular away down south, as they are up here where we can watch four or five of them fly into the air with one accord, above a field of dazzling dandelions on a brilliant sun-drenched day and sing while on the wing their chiming, unforgettable melody.

In the south where bobolinks used to stay awhile before going on to their wintering grounds, they would gang up on the rice fields wherever they could be found and devour such enormous quantities of the precious grain (for its energizing starch, no doubt) that owners of the paddies marched out after the birds with any kind of weapon handy. Growers didn't even dignify the birds with their musical name. They were just plain "ricebirds" to them.

The story of the bobolink's depredations dates back to the era before 1860 when rice was the chief agricultural product of the Carolina coast country. Then the ricebirds, it was said, were responsible for the loss of millions of dollars.

Pilfering flocks were dealt with by plantation hands known as "bird minders" who were stationed at strategic points about the fields, armed with guns, torches and noise-making pans in an effort to scatter the swarming hosts and reduce the losses to the rice crops.

Now that rice is no longer grown in the Carolinas, except where privately planted (and policed), the bird is permitted the status of bobolink. There he is a mere transient who wings his way to the further south without having the epithet of ricebird flung after him. His appearance is undistinguished, his gay summer suit laid away for another year, while his mate is perennially drab and you'd hardly recognize her as a bobolink, either here or there.

There is hardly a leafy tree as summer advances, that does not serve as a stage for the drama of an anxious parent watching over—and encouraging— a partly feathered baby to take its first wing-steps alone.

Take the brilliant redstart—a bird that in full feather resembles the viceroy butterfly, especially in the glamour season when the more colourful male disports his finery to interest a particular lady, by repeatedly expanding (like the butterfly) his gaudy orange and black wings and fanning his red-banded tail.

Fledgelings, when learning to fly, are nearly as big as their parents—the chief difference being in the lack of a tail. And it is a lack! How the poor little things ever achieve flight without the help of so essential a rudder with which to steer, or to balance on the tight-rope, is a mystery. But their wings seem to do double duty, and the speed with which they whip the air suggests the whirr of a hummingbird.

The catbird likes the Russian mulberry, though one I saw ate barberries left on shrubs since the previous fall. Between bites, it sang melodiously. Someone likened its song to Chinese—clever comment, since the vocal ups and downs of the bird resemble the Oriental's musical speech.

All slate grey with cap of darker slate, with its length and slender grace, it is as alert and graceful in its movements as a cardinal. We were taught to call it Canadian mockingbird, but I have not seen this name in any book.

One of my wide-awake readers heard a bird singing on three successive nights, from two o'clock to five a.m. and wondered if it could be a nightingale or a mockingbird. I have never heard of a nightingale in this country. It was probably a Canadian mockingbird which has been known to sing through half the night early in June.

However, I once saw a bird that I was almost certain was a southern mockingbird.

Larger than our catbird, it was greyish with white wing-bar, a noticeably large head, and long trailing tail.

I called the Royal Ontario Museum and told Jim Baillie, an expert on the feathered inhabitants of this area. Mr. Baillie was inclined to agree that we really had seen a mockingbird. They have been known to nest around Toronto, he said, and are definitely extending their territory north into Canada.

The red-eyed vireo may be heard on fine days in every part of Canada where there are trees. Unlike the robin and thrush family, he does not sing in the rain. One of its names is greenlet, from Latin vireo: I am green. It is also called "eyebrow bird" because of the dark line over its eye.

Its nest is suspended below the fork of the tree, never on top of a limb. The vireo is about the only bird to build a pendant nest except the oriole. The nest may be forty feet up, and is woven of grass and lichen, ornamented at times with cocoons and strips of newspaper.

The vireo's sweet disposition causes the tribe to fall easy victim to any roving cowbird that leaves unwanted eggs in other birds' nests. For parent vireos will eagerly feed the young pretenders (hatched from a rover's deposit) even more leaf-rollers than they do their own rightful heirs to the family food. . . . Could be because Baby Cowbird opens its bigger mouth wider, and yells for it louder!

Small as this bird is, there is a sharp little hook at tip of the upper mandible, patterned like the shrike's bill, and useful in spiking spanworms and leaf-rollers. Indeed these small birds are said to eat more of these pests than any other group in feathers. And if a plague of any crawler occurs, they will attack the invaders with vim—and beak. Their song, between gulps of grub, is a monotonous chant of broken phrases.

The red-eyed vireo is olive green above, with no wing-bars, and pearly white below. He has white on side of head with a dark shaft (the "eyebrow") above, and a lesser stripe straight through the eye. The red iris, seen only in a favourable light, is weird when the bird peers at you through varnished leaves. The not-very-long tail is square, instead of forked, at end.

I got a swift glimpse once of its glowing red iris, when the vireo flew into a low branch of our Norwegian ash. Previously the eye had always looked black, and I wondered how the bird ever got its name. Was it slander? Or did the colour come and go like the fire in a wolf's eye?

The vireo is vocal all day—and every day— throughout the summer, regardless of an exploding thermometer. He discourses, in broken phrases, and the pauses seem to give his leaf-hidden congregation time to reflect. Or so thought Wilson Flagg who (said Forbush) gave him the name of "preacher bird."

The great E. H. Forbush, who was a curator of birds in Worcester, Mass., at the age of sixteen, and later became first official State ornithologist of Massachusetts, was led, by this little red-eyed vireo, to a consideration of the economic value of birds.

He observed how the vireo would "scan the foliage," between bars of his singing, then lean forward and snatch a green grub from the under side of a leaf—swallow it—and resume his song. Every important pause signalized the capture of a caterpillar. "As the discourse was punctuated, a worm was punctured," he recorded, and the phrase became a Forbush *bon mot*. Larva hunting—not singing—was the vireo's serious business, he found.

The warbling vireo is a similar bird, paler in colour, but sings a continuous finch-like song. It is just as elusive as the red-eyed vireo and as difficult to see. I have noticed it sing with wings drooping—though I cannot say if this is a regular habit.

Look for the ruby-throated hummingbird when the cardinal flowers are in bloom. It often stays here well into October. This feathered atom— that can sit comfortably in a teaspoon—even drives in the wind as far north as Labrador and sweeps across the edge of the Arctic to the Yukon.

Of the 800 kinds of hummingbirds whirring with jewelled wings among the bright flowers of North and South America (doing seventy whirrs per second) only one species, the ruby-throated hummingbird is adventurous enough to fly up to Eastern Canada, although two species are recorded in the West. British Columbia has the Calliope and the black-chinned. The Calliope is the smallest on this continent.

Next time you sight a Canada goose landing here watch closely. See if it shakes off a little bit of fluff as if it were some irritating insect. Might be a hummingbird!

In the spring of 1943 I rashly released an incredible story of hummers hitch-hiking north on the saddle backs of wild geese. I expected a fusillade. But only one shot was fired.

Dr. A. E. Allin (Fort William) "noted with regret" that we had allowed poetic license to creep in when picturing the hummingbird thumbing a ride north in this manner. "Of course, they do not do so," Dr. Allin charged. "And if they did, where do they stay from the time the geese arrive in March and early April until the hummer is first seen about mid-May?"

However, a letter from W. R. Thornton, of Toronto, stated that he found the tale of that hitch-hiking hummer quite credible.

Mr. Thornton once spent a winter around the James Bay area, where he made the acquaintance of a trapper named Joe, described as a French-Canadian "squaw-man," who had lived there all his life and was a keen observer of nature.

It was Joe who first told him of "dose leedle birds dat ride on de back ov de goose an' fly off when de goose she go to land on de waturr."

As a great many of the geese "summer" up there, he thought Joe's account should be accepted as accurate. Moreover, other people, mostly Indians, had verified Joe's story.

The ruby-throat, whose wings whirl so fast when poised before a flower that they look like wisps of veil flowing from the tiny body, that mere atom with the sturdy breastbone, has the courage and strength to battle a big eagle and make the feathers fly. Rev. J. G. Wood, the English artist-naturalist of a century ago, once saw this happen and recorded it in a drawing.

And yet these fierce little fighters fall a frequent prey to cats that spring from ambush in the foliage while the birds are sipping nectar from flowers near the ground.

I once watched a sharp encounter between a bumblebee and hummingbird. The bee was the attacker, and I would hardly have been more astonished had it started to sing like a lark. Several such battles, seen since, have ended in a draw. Larger birds, like the kingbird, never argue with bees. They simply eat them.

As I have mentioned, holes of the kind made by sapsuckers, that cause the juice of the tree to run, prove a bonanza for the hummer.

Besides gathering the sap, it is possible the hummingbird picks up little insects, though a man I discussed the incident with at the time was of the opinion that hummers ate nothing but nectar. He certainly couldn't credit the idea that anything as dainty as this little feathered jewel would consume anything so repulsive as a bug!

But later I had absolute proof that they would and they do.

While in Quebec, staying at an old-fashioned house where there was a large glassed-in vinery, I picked up a dead hummingbird on the ground inside.

It had evidently flown in one of the open windows and met disaster against the unyielding glass of an opposite closed one. Its beak was clamped on a bunch of small flies and minute spiders, collected no doubt to take to its quota of two baby hummers who must have remained hungry, unless some neighbourly mother of the same species came to the rescue.

The father was off gallivanting. Male hummers never help bring up the young family.

In romantic mood the ruby-throat plays quite a different role. Its courting dance is one of the most charming sights in the bird world. Louise Platt of Moulton College described to me a dance she watched one summer on Lake of Bays.

"We were familiar with hummingbirds around our cabin," Miss Platt told me, "because clumps of bergamot grew there in great profusion . . . and one afternoon we saw a quite unusual performance which was not clear at the time: ruby-throat flew from under the corner of our porch in a great arc of perhaps thirty feet, and swung back and forth over and over, as fast as the eye could follow.

"Suddenly we discovered the reason: A little lady hummer perched on one of the low branches of a near-by balsam. . . . I remember that she seemed quite unimpressed," Louise interpolated, "and very soon she moved on. Though I haven't a doubt that the courtship dance started all over again."

As a postscript she mentioned seeing a hummer thrusting at the red flowers painted on a Chinese lantern on their porch.

If you want to attract hummingbirds, here is a good way. Mrs. George Black, of Whitehorse, told me years ago (when she was living in Dawson) how she had wound bits of scarlet or yellow silk ribbon around little glass test-tubes which she filled with syrup and water, or diluted honey, and hung among the vines screening their veranda. . . . Her idea has since been widely copied.

"Within an hour," Mrs. Black wrote, "I have counted seven tiny humming beauties fluttering about the artificial posies, returning again and again to drain the nectar-filled tubes."

She specified the ruby-throat and one she called golden green, which may have been the Calliope.

Any fine summer day you may hear the cuckoo and, if lucky, see a long, grey-green shape drift down like a feathered leaf into the underbrush. He prefers low thickets, yet on the hottest day of the year one came to our avenue of tall trees and hid behind the green umbrellas of the horse chestnut. He called incessantly through the screen, but you could not tell if he were approving, or protesting, the heat.

The European cuckoo is not a nice bird, though beloved of poets for centuries. It was called by Virgil the "vagrant cuckoo"— classic term for philanderer.

If you are one of those busybodies, like a little girl I knew once upon a time, who like to manage the affairs of birds, don't try the cuckoo. This child of seven had been told (by her father) of an English cuckoo that had the bad habit of laying one of its eggs in another bird's nest. She was also shown a picture.

In their Picton garden one day, the small girl noticed a few sticks shaped like a nest in a wild apple tree. So she watched, and along came a bird (that looked like the picture) and began to add sticks to the nest.

The little self-made warden got a bigger stick and put the bird to rout, then boasted later to her father that she had "chased away a naughty cuckoo."

Her parent gently hinted that she was the naughty one, and explained patiently that the kind of cuckoos we had in Canada were respectable birds who built and furnished their own nests, and she should not have driven the bird away.

You've guessed it . . . that naughty little girl was me!

The black-billed cuckoo, and its close relative, the yellow-billed, have long, graceful tails evident in flight. Fuzzy caterpillars are their favourite food, notably the horrid tent caterpillars.

And Taverner records in his *Birds of Canada* how the lining of a cuckoo's stomach is coated with spiny bristles of the caterpillar, almost as thick as fur. A case of the skin-side inside. Moreover, this does not seem to hurt the birds. Indeed, it may act as a filter in lieu of liver.

At Ward's Island (October 15, 1939) I had a grand view of a yellow-billed cuckoo. Its lower mandible is deep yellow—the primrose stain running over the feathers of the bird's full throat, in pretty contrast to its oyster-white breastplate. Its upper bill has a decided curve and its wings are washed with British tan. The long, dark tail, so graceful in flight, is evenly notched with white, and the bird has very dark eyes.

It does not say "coo-coo" like its European namesake, or our black-billed cuckoo. Someone has likened its music to "the sound of a loose-mouthed hound lapping from a pan of milk." A sort of glug! glug! But my yellow-billed cuckoo sang enchantingly at Ward's Island between bites of tent caterpillars!

And during these eventful weeks, while hundreds of small voyagers have been arriving daily from the south on the wings of vagrant winds and fanning out in different directions to find space for suitable nesting sites, there has been a definite outgoing movement of what we have come to know as the winter birds. Taking the hint, perhaps, that their places here were wanted.

Chickadees, kinglets, downy woodpeckers, the blue and white nuthatch and the odd grosbeak are on the march, beaks pointing north to sniff the evergreens.

Birds that spent many inclement nights hereabout, crouched in shelter-nests or some tree hollow, would come out by day to munch whatever food they could find—mountain ash berries, the sumac's purple velvet beads, and the winged pendants of Manitoba maples. Or, whenever tempted, landing for dinner at a friendly feeding station.

The Nutcracker Suite, as I like to call it, has been assembling in restless flocks for the journey north to the limits of the timberline, to the land of "the murmuring pines and the hemlocks."

They usually start the flight about dusk, their little music boxes silent for the night, to be unwound at dawn when the birds begin to drop down out of the sky after a "lookout" has flashed the signal that there are lots of cone-bearing trees below and a happy landing place.

3. Voices of the Marsh

Rails, Red-winged Blackbirds, Bitterns,
Gallinules, Herons, Egrets, Woodcocks,
Black Terns

IF YOU HAVE BEEN MISLED into thinking a marsh
just a smelly place to agitate against, then go out to
the nearest pond some fine evening soon and sniff
for yourself.   There is a very good chance that you
will find the air redolent of nothing more odorif-
erous than balm of Gilead, varied by sweet whiffs
of the blossoming basswood, sometimes called the
bee-tree because, while it's in flower, thousands
of wild bees clamour for foothold to glean the
nectar. . . . It is a thing to remember, just to
stand under a basswood tree and listen to the
honeyed humming of a myriad glistening wings in
the leafy rafters.

Go out to your nearest marsh, then, and
discover, through glasses, the lone bittern in partial
eclipse among the old-gold reeds.   Listen to the
measured tick-tick of the gallinule.   Watch the
roistering redwings in a clever balance act as they
cling to the bending bulrushes, or try to imitate the
whinny of a slender rail.

You have heard the phrase, "Thin as a rail."
The reference was not to a fence rail (as I had once

45

RAIL

thought) but to that funny, bob-tailed bird of the marshes which has to be thin in order to squeeze its homeward way through those narrow spaces between the stiff canes where it lives.

There has been a succession of Virginia rails nesting at Grenadier Pond, Toronto, but they are only half the size of the king rail.

This rail dates back to the renowned Audubon who first discovered the king. He also discovered the rough-wing swallow, facts related in that notable book, *South Carolina Bird Life* (by Sprunt and Chamberlain). A flock of rough-wings was hunting insects last Sunday over the very pond that harboured this rare rail. There also were lots of tree swallows and I saw one purple martin.

Audubon was tall and slim, with an eye like an eagle for making sight records, so he was the logical discoverer of an elusive marsh bird that hid among the rushes.

Another noted ornithologist (Forbush) wrote that, owing to its retiring habits, little was known of the king rail except that it preferred fresh to salt marshes. He confessed that he himself never had seen one alive.

46

The king rail had not been recorded in Toronto, ever, so far as we know. . . . Taverner, Canadian authority, says the species "is too rare in Canada except in the more southern parts of Ontario, to be recorded on eyesight alone." (Mine was helped by a pair of French field-glasses.)

So you may imagine how the sight of that lovely buffy-breasted bird, peering with gentle eyes from its retreat half hidden by a greening fringe at the edge of a little island in Catfish Pond, sent my heart zooming.

And when king rail swung his long beak and stepped cautiously from cover, bobbed across a small area of sandy beach, then waded right in and swam out into the perilous pond—that brought the ultimate thrill to this bird watcher.

The call of the rail has been likened to human laughter. The Virginia rail, which summers here, can afford to laugh, because it haunts and hides in secluded marshlands, evading its enemies quite effectively.

Lucky is the farmer on whose damp meadows the Virginia rail settles, for the bad "army worms" breed there—those caterpillars that can march in such vast hordes to devastate any field over which they pass. This little nine-inch bird devours the enemy with gusto, and also helps to check horse-flies and other pests that swarm the "haunts of coot and hern."

The rail's bill is longer than its head. It has a very short tail, long strong legs and long toes. Its flattened form permits the bird to thread its way among the reeds, also to dive.

RED-WINGED BLACKBIRDS

The long toes serve them to foot-it over the soft mud. Their small wings are little used except in migration. Their breast and back are cinnamon; the under parts are white streaked with dark wavy bands. One name is "little mudhen."

Their nest is a rude bulky platform of dried bulrushes. The young arrive covered with black down, they can scamper and swim as soon as hatched. The babies have enormous feet for their size, making them look like little music-stands.

Fraternizing with the rail is the red-winged blackbird whose voice has an almost thrush-like quality as it flutes its melody over marshes, oka-ree! . . . oka-ree! . . . oka-ree! . . . Redwings ride in on the first wave of spring migration and "wherever there are streams and ponds, this handsome, rollicking redwing will be found."

Lady Redwing, in dusky stripes and white-bordered calotte, is regarded by some as finer than her mate in spite of the red dazzle of his military epaulettes on parade.

The redwing is charged with "gorging itself on wild rice till not a grain is left, thereby depriving wild ducks, etc., of a most attractive food." Now

48

I ask you, is not the redwing as good as any duck? Then how about sowing more wild rice (instead of oats) so there'll be enough to go around? Dr. W. T. Hornaday once said: "It is men—not the animals—who are wild."

The stage was set—late afternoon one May Day, beside the marshy end of Grenadier Pond, waiting for a bittern to appear. I knew the bird was there, some place, for every few minutes that queer gurgle of sound came from the reeds, more like a bullfrog than a bird, and variously described as stake-driving, pump-priming, or booming.

Really it was the bittern's wedding song! Only the male sings, and just at this time of year when he is looking for a mate.

A lowering sun filtered through the haze, burnishing the dull-gold rushes and flecking the surface of narrow channels that wound among the reeds. Red-winged blackbirds flew in and out of the marsh, now and again alighting to swing on a tall stalk, the sunlight accenting their red-and-orange epaulettes, while they chattered happily over their nesting plans, and sang the familiar "Oka-ree! Oka-ree! Oka-ree!"

A quiver in the reeds indicated where to turn my field-glasses and in time to see the bittern step out of hiding, dressed in his wedding finery of soft buff feathers. Brown wavy stripes trailed from his throat down the front of the waistcoat, with two dark patches pendant from either side of beak. Something special were the clusters of chalk-white

BITTERN

nuptial plumes that curled outward from each shoulder.

The bittern's keen bright eye—red in some lights—blinked a couple of times, before he began that queer dance which precedes the song, a wriggling of the whole body so that the stripes wriggled, too. Then he drew himself up to look tall, and very dignified.

It was a pose. For dignity was shattered when he began to sing. First he opened his long mandibles as though to yawn, and clapped them together, producing the sound of a small mallet tapping lightly on wood, fancifully called stake-driving. The bird did this three times.

Next came the famous pumping—a realistic rendition of the priming of a farmer's old wooden pump. I actually heard the water coming up!

To produce this sound (which Forbush has interpreted as "plunk-a-lunk") the bittern would throw the head forward, with staccato jerk, before each three-syllable croak, then slap down its beak as if trying to shake a slug off the tip. The song was about as musical as the cry of a man who sells kindling along our avenue, when he calls "Whooo-awd! Whooo-awd!" as though he were about to be sick at sea. And the sight was as pretty as that of a snake trying to swallow a too-big frog.

The bittern may have caught sight of the field-glasses and mistaken them for owl's eyes. For the bird suddenly froze into his stick-like posture and remained stiff for ten minutes (by my watch) without turning a feather. The only sign of life I could detect was the occasional blink of a bright eye.

The knight of the fen is a solitary fellow, generally alone except when a mate is attracted by his weird love-song. He frequents stagnant pools flanked by old-gold rushes which serve as camouflage when it stiffens its body and points beak straight up to look like a clump of the reeds.

In contrast, the smallest of the species, the least bittern, has a mellow cooing note, not unlike a mourning dove, and far removed from the mal-de-mer of the big marshbird.

The least bittern measures about eight inches, in the crouched position. But when drawing itself to full height in order to look like a reed (for which it hopes to be mistaken) it may reach a foot. It has slim head and neck, a black slender cap, blackish back and buffy wing-patches.

It climbs easily among the bulrushes and may be seen clinging to a reed, like the marsh wren.

Alexander Sprunt describes the bittern as one of the most protectively coloured of birds. "The bittern (he records) can be gazed upon at very short range and still not be seen. Head and neck erect, it stands like a brown statue among the reeds, and it will actually sway with the waving grasses if a breeze is blowing. When suddenly flushed it springs upward with a guttural croak and flies away like a brown phantom."

A bittern can get itself into a greater variety of queer shapes and postures than almost any bird I know. Though generally represented in books as tall, stick-like, erect, with slender neck and a stiff bill pointing straight up to the zenith, it has appeared to me more often in absolute denial of a neck—all hunched and bunched and bristling like a fretful porcupine.

I find little recorded of the seasonal meanderings of the bittern. Some have been found wintering as far away as Panama and the West Indies, though the majority evidently loiter around the marsh-lands of the Southern States.

They straggle south from Ontario in late September and early October and, if you happen to see them off, note how their heads are hunched back against the shoulders and long legs trailing out behind, after the manner of the heron tribe.

Their flight is so leisurely and the bird on the wing presents such an easy target to the casual gun-toter that many a fine bittern has been left languishing among the reeds—not even retrieved, it is said.

Related species inhabit many parts of the world. There is a black bittern in the Solomon Islands, and an Australian variety that wanders to other islands in the Southwest Pacific. The Chinese least bittern has been seen in the Marianas. It is twelve inches long, a trifle smaller than the kind found on Toronto Island.

Gallinules, normally marsh dwellers and birds that love to get their funny long feet wet and keep them that way, may appear during migration in the most fantastic situations and the driest places.

The uttermost was reached when a Florida gallinule was found early the other morning at the bottom of a five-foot can outside Cornell Engineering Works. The gallinule may have been heading for Grenadier Marsh, for there are many Florida gallinules in the marshes near Toronto. A record in my diary (June 11, 1949) notes a thrill I got when watching one of these birds, which are supposed to

53

be very secretive, come out in full view, to take a bath in Grenadier Pond where they nest.

A penetrating tick-tick, tick-tick, repeated regularly, indicated that a gallinule was on the march. So I swept every foot of the terrain with my fieldglasses and watched from a comfortable cushion of grass on the west bank overlooking the pond.

Presently, out from a clump of border reeds came the handsome, dark, twelve-inch bird, its fiery red beak and high frontal bone glowing in the sun.

It stepped out cautiously, continually pecking food from the mud flats. Then wading into one of the narrow channels between the sand bars, the bird swam along, giving its peculiar forward head-thrust with every stroke of its splayed paddles.

Then what luck! The gallinule decided to take a bath. It turned west and, crossing three channels, tiptoed to the waterlane nearest to my lookout, where it splashed luxuriously for fully five minutes, then emerged to dry its feathers and preen in the sun. At intervals it stopped this routine to shake its white-tipped feather bustle, a modern ballet touch, and once lifted a long-toed foot to scratch behind its ear.

On another day a family party of Florida gallinules disported on the sand bars in Grenadier marsh. Birds which every book on our shelf declared secretive were in view most of the afternoon. And for the first time in my life, save in pictures, I was lucky enough to see the cute little gallinules.

There were two adults, bantam-size, with

black coats, red beaks and matching red garters to hold up their long green stockings. And in the offing, five little blackish babies with noses red as their dad's.

Unlike baby ducks, the small gallinules were not strictly herded, but allowed to scamper around at will, even run and hide among the tall green rushes. And the parents didn't seem worried, as mother ducks do.

Four of the five youngsters—they were only about as big as toy Easter chicks—would wade into the pool and swim without any urging from the grownups. But the fifth, equally large, stayed put, either lacking enterprise, courage, or the wit to go and do likewise.

Mother Gallinule tried to stir the reluctant one into action. It was fun to watch her, as she would run with short wings flapping, straight at the little bird as though to attack it, but stop short. Then turn about and run splashing into the pool as if to say, "Come in. The water's fine!"

But the small bird remained stolid, muttering, it seemed, "Splash in the puddle all you like. Me, I stand here 'n' watch you. It's too much exertion on a hot day." And the old bird soon tired of trying.

The last time we heard gallinules calling was in June, at mating time, when the bird's note was quite different—a sharp "tick! tick!" You'd hardly recognize the voice now, unless you saw the bird. The soft, sweet clucking sounds which bring the baby gallinules running to either parent for food picked out of the mud flat and transferred to the first little beak to arrive.

55

The marsh is the place to see herons and the whole tribe of long-legged waders is extremely interesting.

First thing I had to learn years ago when observing the green heron (smallest member of the heron family) was that it didn't appear to be green at all, but a dull blue. . . . I find John Kieran in his *Introduction to Birds* (Doubleday) puzzled about the same thing.

Mr. Kieran flatly asks, "Why green heron?" adding that, "To most observers it shows more slate-blue or an even darker shade on most of the upper plumage." He does admit, however, that its crown is green.

It has short yellow legs, fierce ruby eyes, a terrific beak out of all proportion to bird's size, and says "quawk" when it wants to attract the attention of a frog. It habitually hunches its shoulders in a regular slouch, though it draws itself up and flips open its crest if alarmed. The iridescent green coat may appear blue in certain lights—my sole excuse for misidentifying one at the Island some years ago, as a little blue heron.

While watching three green herons that hunted from three separate pitches in Catfish Pond at High Park, I did see a spot of green on the nose, though it was not very definite. And one of the three had not much blue showing either. It had on a rough overmantle of brownish hue that could have been the "eclipse" plumage which some birds affect during the late summer. About the size of a fish crow, it seems to shrink to kingfisher size when it wants to remain unobserved.

The green heron seldom nests in colonies like the big herons, each pair going off to some quiet nook near water. A tamarack was chosen to house the basket of eggs, which I saw and they were green, too!

I saw something quite unusual one day. One of the green herons did a slanting dive into the pond from his perch on an anchored log, whirled about in the water and was back in two shakes with a fish or small frog in his beak. . . . I didn't know it was unusual until I happened to read about a similar incident in Forbush after I got home.

Most fascinating of all herons I find to be the black-crowned night heron; the adult bird—not junior which is an ungainly creature, and looks as though a curry comb might improve his coiffure and also serve to scrape off those white pendant doo-dads that resemble some of the things we hang on Christmas trees. The young have staring yellow eyes that turn red as the birds grow older, possibly from many months of night prowling.

The adult has greenish-black cap, white face and breast and blue-grey wings, with two fine white plumes falling over the dark, pointed cape. Both have heavy sharp beak and big feet. Showy tan and white stripes mark the young herons which are sometimes mistaken for bitterns. But they shouldn't be, for though about the same size, they are of quite a different shape and stance. Moreover, bitterns crouch among the cattails in marshy places. I've never seen one set foot in a tree, and that's where herons usually congregate.

In 1950, we in Toronto discovered a night-blooming heronry right at our own front door. It was on the one uninhabited island in the Toronto chain across the bay, a fact these uncanny birds must have discovered.

I arrived at the landing just before sunset and had hardly stepped ashore when the noisy chorus began of the young birds with their thin quacks (either of alarm or hunger) mingled with solo parts in the deep bass of adults uttering what sounded like "walk! . . . walk!"

The willows were furnished with many big loosely constructed nests of sticks, none of which appeared to be occupied. The young had crawled out onto the limbs and were perched here and there while scores of older herons were cutting beautiful capers of flight above the trees.

Night herons feed their young mostly on fish, so don't go too near a heronry if the scent of ancient fish offends your nostrils. The Toronto Island parents would fly to the beach and pick up half-dead shad that were floating along the bay shore and carry them back in their beaks to the crying baby herons who are not very fussy about what they eat.

Their clutch consists of three to five eggs and the nests were a loose arrangement of sticks, so loose you would think that eggs might fall through the openings. We did find many eggshells scattered on the ground of a chalk-blue colour and rough texture. Also lots of moulted feathers blown about.

We did not arrive at the rookery in time to see

the night heron's ritual dance. But according to Roger Tory Peterson (in *Birds Over America*) and Bob Allen who understands bird psychology, these birds develop bright coral legs during courtship.

Males, each on his own territory, begin the Beguine (a set routine of bowing and scraping) and soon the whole colony is caught up in the spirit of the thing.

Lady night herons approach the calling males, timidly, to be accepted (or rebuffed) according to the pitch of colour—indicating maturity—reached by their nylon stockings in the dyeing process. If only a pale yellow, the young debs have to go away and dip them again. . . . "Bird psychology is a baffling thing!" Mr. Peterson comments.

During my visit to the little island, a pair of stately great blue herons, alarmed in their quiet fishing by the commotion among the night herons caused by our invasion of their nursery, leaped into the air with long legs swinging like a pendulum until height and balance were attained, folded their long elastic necks back into their shoulders and flapped out across the island southward where they let down their landing gear at a safe distance from the disturbed area.

An interesting "discovery" came to me in a letter signed H. J. C. about great blue herons—"that they will land on deep water." It was news to me. At Wellington (Prince Edward County) last summer, H. J. C. heard this, but he "had his doubts." A few days later he was convinced.

Watching a flock of herons about a quarter mile off shore, he noted that they "would alight on the water, retrieve a fish, or whatever food was there, and then after a few minutes, rise easily and continue their search for more food."

H. J. C. (who is an engineer) spent nearly three years on the construction of the air base at Goose Bay, Labrador, and there "saw a few herons." He has "since wondered how much further north they really go."

Curator L. L. Snyder (when queried) stated that the great blue heron "nests regularly as far north as the height of land in Ontario—from Temiskaming to Kenora—and that, like all other herons, it performs a post-nesting, wandering flight—often north of its breeding area—and has been observed as far north as Fort Severn on Hudson Bay."

Curator Snyder lent support to H. J. C.'s discovery that the great blue heron does swim, by his own observation during a faunal investigation at Long Point, near Port Rowan, Lake Erie. Mr. Snyder saw a heron alight on the open bay, about 200 yards off shore, when "its appearance, and behaviour, after alighting on the water, was gull-like. The wings were carefully folded, and the set of its head and neck suggested the bird was floating, not standing." And he added that from soundings he took from a punt, "the bird could not have been resting on the bottom, but was floating." The curator watched it "take off without difficulty and settle a second time on the water."

I have since found further confirmation in an old book, written in 1875, by J. G. Wood—a British naturalist—who, while describing the black stork

60

of Palestine, remarked that "it was never seen to swim, as the heron sometimes does."

Before the time of William IV, the heron was protected by law, because of its value in sport and as food. An act was passed, in James I's reign, making it illegal "to shoot with any gun within 600 paces of a heronry." Strange logic! They were sparing the heron's life to be sacrificed to the falcon.

The American egret belongs to the same family as the great blue heron. It stands four feet tall, and its entire plumage is white as a snow-drift. The long bill is pale gold. Its legs and feet are black as coal; the eyes golden yellow.

It was on August 18, 1947, that I watched the egret at Centre Island, for an hour, mostly around the then-flooded area north of the tennis court and wildfowl pond. I first noticed the big white bird trying to settle on a too-slim branch of the willow at the edge of the north lagoon. It changed its mind, lifted silken wings and folded back its long slender neck against the shoulders (in true heron fashion) pointed its long yellow beak, then flapped leisurely inland over the flooded field. Lowering its black legs among the reeds and wet grass, the egret spied and spiked several juicy morsels during that hour.

Nobody seems to know why, but it is only the young egret that wanders up here at this time of year. Sheer rebellion, or a natural urge to see the world, may impel these full-grown youngsters to snap family ties in late summer, lift their lovely white parasols and undulate in this direction, until they sight a likely place to land.

They come down to earth both literally and figuratively and stand patiently for hours in wet places watching for any chance frog or silver shiner to be speared with their yellow javelin. And though the protesting creature is swallowed without much grace (either whole if small enough, or in bits and pieces), the bird is storing up energy in vitamins, for the return journey south when our early frosts remind them of a shrinkage in the food supply here and that they had better turn their feather prows towards the Florida Everglades.

The beauty of this white heron recalls the old Greek legend of the heron's curious origin,—How Aeneas, the Trojan hero, went to Italy to make a new home for the remnant of his people, and was opposed by Turnus of Ardea, who burned Aeneas' ships. In the resulting battle, Turnus was slain and the Trojans set fire to Ardea, the king's chief city. When Ardea was burned to the ground, a queer bird—the heron—arose from the embers and beat the ashes with its flapping wings. The new bird, then listed for the first time, was described as having "the voice, the leanness, the paleness and everything that befits a captured city," even to its classic name, Ardea.

Picture a velvet April dusk . . . following a flaming sunset that sweeps across the heavens in a tidal wave of colour, rolling into ridges of shocking pink . . . like coral reefs in a turbulent sea of turquoise—more green than blue. . . . And you have your atmosphere.

Then listen! . . . If you are lucky—and are out in high rubber boots at the edge of a dismal swamp or nice gooey bog—you may hear the wedding song of the woodcock.

Two or three stars are out. First you hear a harsh, ascending note, "Zeep!" . . . Then the same sound, but dragged a bit, like "Ze . . . ee . . . eep!" repeated over and over again, a few seconds apart, as from a bird strutting in the field. Then, just before the takeoff, the sibilant sound is uttered more rapidly and at shorter intervals.

If you have been fairly close to the warming-up sounds of his engine, you will be near the woodcock's circle of flight, and see him pass. Can watch him take the air and hear his quick, incessant chittering—rather musical—as the shadowy bird goes up and up on a spiral ladder into the mysterious dusk. Then a dramatic descent.

You cannot quite see the landing, but he is probably picking himself up. The zeeping begins all over again. A second climb into the sky is made and another flight-song is set spinning through the upper air. And this amazing performance goes on and on, until the bird's wings and his throat are tired—or the mate in hiding calls time.

Big eyes and forest snipe are but two of the many names applied in various localities to this prince of protective colouration, the oak-brown mottled woodcock. . . . And it has always seemed a bit surprising that he should be listed among the shore birds. I have never encountered one anywhere near a beach.

They revel in boggy places along the edge of some nice swamp where they can bury that long, nimble spoon in the mud and bring up a protesting, juicy worm at almost every dip.

Their names are not mere aliases. Each conveys a meaning. . . . Not only has the woodcock big eyes, but outlandish ears that are curiously extended which may be connected with its feeding methods.

The true ears of the feathered tribe are generally behind and below the eyes. But in the woodcock they are not only below but also in front of the (big) eyes, and the large "auditory bulbae" indicate that their owner "listens" for movements of its underground quarry in the waterlogged soil.

The bird is classed with the snipes. One name is whistling snipe. Others are timber doodle, hookum pake, and big eyes. Still another, bogsucker, indicates the kind of ground the woodcock haunts, which will be found full of holes called "borings."

Thousands of birds perished during a recent severe winter down South, when the ground was so hard that no borings could be made through which to pull up the worms for food. The bird's upper mandible can be flexed like a finger to "feel" for the worms.

If you go to the edge of a swamp on a spring evening you may come across a patch of boggy ground punched full of holes as though some one

64

had been prodding the muck with a cane. A nesting bird is probably not far away.

Now look at the woodcock's nest. There are four eggs, and observers have found that, for some reason, they are always arranged with the small ends pointed toward the centre.

Then watch for the sprightly antics of her brown mottled mate as he performs his aerial song and dance, especially enchanting if it happens to be moonlight. He flutters from the ground in mothlike manner, then spirals up into the twilit sky to a height of fifty or sixty feet while he sings, and tumbles, and sings—for her alone.

The common tern loves the open water as a gull does but the black tern is different. It goes for the marshlands every time. It builds loosely woven egg-holders, of dried grasses—floating generally, though anchored to the surface vegetation or placed perhaps on top of a muskrat's lodge. The eggs are greyish green and almost covered with brown freckles.

In afternoon or early evening you may see flocks of seven or eight hunting over the marsh, pairs nesting among the reeds.

Look for slate-grey birds, like the catbird in colour and deepening to black on the head and neck, about ten inches in length from tip of beak to end of forked tail and with long pointed wings extending far beyond the tail. Their flight, in its sharp wing-twists and swift turns, is not unlike that of the nighthawk.

The terns cry incessantly. Some say they

scream. But to us it sounds more like a curious elongated chirp, not unmusical.

They stop in their flight every minute or so to hover, then turn their beak sharply down, as if pointing at something they want to strike, and dive to get whatever it is—probably an insect. This is hawking.

Their food consists chiefly of marsh insects, such as dragonflies and moths or water beetles. Though they will snap up any minnow or killifish that may happen to glint across their sharp field of vision, the black tern preys on no marketable fish, takes nothing that you might want for breakfast.

Books give this bird the secondary name of sea swallow, though it might more suitably be called pond swallow. For we doubt if these terns have ever seen the sea, or are ever likely to unless possibly during migration when they fly south to winter in Central or South America. Out on the Canadian prairies they could be called slough swallows. There are lots of black terns out there.

4. Wings over the Water

Ducks, Grebes, Loons, Cormorants, Gulls,
Terns, Gannets, Wild Geese, Swans

JULY IS THE MONTH when you may see on island
lagoons or marshy flats through the country, little
detachments of ducklets being convoyed by an
anxious and extremely vigilant mother duck.

It is always the duck that not only broods the
nestlings, but leads them around and brings them
to maturity—excepting those that fall by the
wayside to some devouring fish or greedy bullfrog.
And while the family is little, the mother duck
chases the drake away whenever he comes too near,
for he has been known to attack the babies,
through jealousy of the duck's devotion to her
brood and her consequent neglect of Mr. Drake.

Mrs. J. B. Stewart, the secretary of the Toronto
Field Naturalists' Club, was one of a canoe party
going down Bella Lake, seventeen miles north of
Huntsville, when they saw an American merganser
swimming along with nine ducklets in tow. And
when the mother saw their canoe approaching, she
hurried her little flock in a different direction.

But one infant that either seemed to think the
fleet was not moving fast enough, or else because
its little paddles were tiring, hopped up onto its

mother's broad back and hitch-hiked for the rest of the journey, Mrs. Stewart related.

A brooding duck plucks the finest feathers from her own breast and weaves them into a comforter for the cradle, so that when she has occasion to leave, either for food or exercise, she can pull up the downy blanket and cover the nest—not only to protect her precious eggs from a chill, but from marauders in fur or feathers. The idea of eider-down quilts for human beds was borrowed (or stolen) from this habit of wild ducks.

Known around the world is the mallard. He might be called grand-daddy of the duck tribe, for he is reputed ancestor of every important variety of domestic duck. So he is a peer of the jungle fowl, to which all barnyard chickens owe their origin.

Mallards may be seen any day—winter or summer—along Ontario waterways. A bright green head, gold bill, and sharp white feathers at rear, that can spread into a small fantail beneath the crisp black hind-curl, are field marks of the drake. The duck, while not showy like her mate, has a quack he can hear a mile away—when she wants him home. He answers meekly: "Queep!... queep! . . . coming!"

A Wards Islander reported that one day she saw a mother mallard round up her baby band of ten, on the lagoon, and "quack" them out onto the safety of the beach, away from the submarine menace of bullfrogs and fishes. For a lively big fish had got one of the little brood, grabbed the ducklet by its leg and drew it under to make a meal. Frogs have been seen behaving like that fish, and with equal success.

The duck that is called the black duck is dusky brown with lighter mottled neck, has a greenish bill and coral feet. It is a kind of black mallard, though less easy to tame than the greenhead. In fact, the black duck is said to be incurably wild. It ranges Southern and Eastern Canada up into Labrador; but is not common west of the Great Lakes; likes thick bushy swamps and reedy bogs for nesting, and the willow is its favourite tree. The nest, difficult to discover without an eagle eye, is large and well constructed, with a deep cup— quilted as described above.

My most vivid memory of the wood duck dates back to a call from a bird watcher one October to tell me that a wood duck—perhaps the most beautiful duck in the world—was swimming on one of the Island lagoons, its startling beauty leaping at you from among its escort that included a number of handsome male mallards. As he said, it looked more like a "carved ornament" than a live bird, with its queer green helmet, purple-studded breastplate, fawn sides, rust patches and striking white lines.

There have been years of controversy among naturalists as to how baby wood ducks, born in the heart of a tree twenty to forty feet from the ground, get down to earth and toddle off after mother duck to the nearest water hole, maybe a hundred yards away from their nesting site.

For the wood duck, when it wants to nest, dives into a hole in the side of a gnarled tree and they say it carries the ducklings one by one in its stout bill to the nearest water for their first swim.

This pretty theory was shattered for me when Dr. Walter J. Breckenridge of Minneapolis showed in Toronto by moving pictures, how the little downy ducklings poke their heads, one by one, out of the nesting cavity and simply tumble to the ground, apparently without injury.

He laughed at the old idea that Mother Woodies either picked the nestlings up in their web feet, or carried them on their backs, to the nearest pond.

I felt he proved this beyond question as the audience in Eaton Auditorium breathlessly watched twenty-four baby wood ducks one after another (and once two together) popping out of a high hole in the basswood tree to the ground, at the call of Mother Duck.

But when I reported on this visual proof that the newly hatched youngsters just jumped out of the nest cavity high up in a tree, and took the consequences, a Toronto doctor sent me another theory of the method by which wood ducklings leave the nest, differing from this filmed story.

The doctor quotes Archibald Rutledge, in *Home by the River*, in which he said that "Suddenly the mother wood duck—how beautiful and gentle were her movements— stooped over the nest, picked up one of the young in her bill, lifted it carefully, held it clear of the limb and over the water just a few feet below, selecting (I could tell) a safe place on which her baby could fall—and then dropped it. The little black ball shot downward, landed with an elfin splash in the water, immediately righted itself, and began to paddle about gaily and happily.

"And in this precise manner," Rutledge added, "the mother deftly and warily dropped from the nest the entire brood."

The little ones were about the size of baby chicks, and black. And when the brood of nine was in the water, the mother wood duck, "with a delicious note of relief and contentment," settled there herself.

Suddenly naturalist Rutledge "became aware" of the gorgeous male duck which must have been near all the time. "He came swimming out of a patch of marsh and wampee, joined his family, and moved quietly and gracefully off into the lagoon."

An Island scout sent us a flash one winter day about some white ducks he had seen in Blockhouse Bay and in the outer lagoon at Centre Island. White ducks with black heads he said they were and seemed quite excited.

He got us excited, too. So I went over on the icebreaker, which made its way through sheets of thin, tinkling ice, and investigated the white duck mystery. In the outer lagoon was a mixed flock of forty to fifty ducks, and through glasses I picked out several which might have misled the scout. For in their brilliant winter dress, the drakes sported lots of white.

First, the handsome coween, riding the waves like a clipper. Absurdly called "Old Squaw," the books record the misnomer. Why, nobody seems to know, though the Indian name coween is much nicer and more musical.

These ducks are called also old-wives and long-tailed ducks. They make a brilliant show with their black and white coats. The males are distinctive, having two pointed tail-feathers projecting several inches beyond their tail proper and slightly up-tilted.

Another conspicuously white duck was the buffle-head (called butter-ball because he looks it) with white flange at side of head bearing a slight resemblance to the hooded merganser. And his hull is all white, even below the plimsoll line. He can dive, too, like a little loon, and playfully slides over the water, on descending from a flight, like those Florida gals on water-skis.

Third was golden-eye, distinguished by large white polka-dot between his yellow orb and base of bill. His hull is all white, too. And I saw one Barrow's golden-eye very similar, but in place of polka-dot, he showed the silver crescent, like a young winter moon.

All of the above might be casually called white ducks while in winter dress.

On another such trip I got a terrific thrill when, midway between the city docks and Hanlan's Point, there appeared off the port side a specimen of that king among waterfowl, a canvasback duck, and the first one I have ever seen on Toronto Bay.

Called "cans" for short, these birds are swift on the wing, expert divers and hard to retrieve. They breed around Great Slave Lake and on to Alaska.

In a stiff sou'wester it was rocking along the waves and so close to the ferryboat that my field glasses were not necessary. There was a breathless moment when the bird nearly bumped into the boat—but the thrill changed to chagrin when I suddenly saw that the thing was a wooden duck!

It was so nicely carved and coloured, that it looked like Allan Brook's painting of the canvas-back—a big oyster-white body, rich red head and neck, low forehead, ruby eyes and a long wedgelike bill.

Mystery surrounds that wooden duck—not to be confused with the wood duck! Why was it there in the middle of Toronto Bay? Where had it been before dragging its anchor and drifting into the ferry traffic lanes? Would any one come to claim the decoy?

No one would dare. Though finders might be keepers, the wooden duck could be "confiscated" by some one who happened to find it "out of bounds."

An even subtler decoy well known to hunters, the call duck is a small, white, trim duck with short, yellow bill, yellow feet, and dark eyes. Named for their continuous "call," which carries a long distance, "they are admirable decoys to allure the wild species of ducks to their destruction," says a breeder.

The pied-billed grebe is a wee waterfowl that looks like a duck but isn't. It is not as large even as the green-winged teal which a Toronto authority, F. H. Kortright, lists as "the smallest of our wild fowl."

Though a straight flier, and fairly fast, the pied-bill is not quick on the turn, owing possibly to its sawed-off tail. In fact, it could hardly be called slanderous to say this grebe has no tail at all!

Young grebes can swim almost as soon as they shed their shells. And a mother grebe has been known to take four or five babies under her wings, dive and swim with them to a safer place to bring them up, some fifty feet away from the anchored nest.

One fine October day I watched two pied-billed grebes who were swimming, with heads erect, their light "hulls" glistening in the sun with a metallic lustre. Occasionally one of the grebes would furtively lower its body beneath the surface and remain submerged (while danger seemed to threaten), with only its beak sticking up and one eye visible—a perfect periscope! At other times, it would openly dive for food. The grebe has a smooth, straight, compressed bill—best kind for diving—and with linear nostrils.

If you've ever watched a dabchick or other small grebe on some marshy pond remain under water ever so long with only its beak pointed up among the pickerel weeds, you will get the idea which the inventor of that Snorkel breathing apparatus had in mind. He probably filched the idea from the ingenious grebe.

When alarmed, the grebe sinks slowly down and swims beneath the surface until it reaches the weedy patches where it stays submerged with only its beak above the waterline. So long as it can breathe like the snorkel, the grebe knows it's safe.

Least of the grebe family (about thirteen inches), the eared grebe is slightly smaller than the horned grebe, from which it differs by a black neck and (in summer) by a flashy pair of blonde ear-muffs that flatten back against the grebe's cheeks like fringed seashells. A tapering dark helmet juts up from the forehead, lending grace and balance.

They have Chinese red flanks, and their lobed feet are built for quick paddle-strokes. They can dive like—well, if you know their nickname,* you'll know what!

Eared grebes inhabit reedy edges of sloughs on the Canadian prairies and it is said they often gather in such close-packed colonies that a slender canoe can only with difficulty be pushed along between the lines of their floating nests.

The loon, finely patterned with checkered back and brilliant necklace, swims low in water and dives to amazing depths.

Loons build their nests of moss, seaweed, and twigs on an island and near the shore so they can haul themselves out of the water readily, and also, when alarmed, slide back into the water like a turtle. The loon carefully turns her two very dark brown eggs. The idea of chocolate eggs may have had its origin in one of her bulky nests.

The loon is helpless on land, according to L. L. Snyder, an authority at the museum. It cannot take off from solid ground because of the way its legs are attached—much like the rear flippers of a seal.

These divers feed on fish, which they pursue and capture under water. I watched a loon one

* Hell-Diver

summer playing with a fish in Lake Ontario off the mouth of the Rouge River. He brought up a shining fellow from one of his diving forays and kept flipping it over his back and then into the water again, ever so often, until the fish finally gave up the struggle and slid down the bird's throat. Mr. Snyder says the loon has a distensible gullet capable of taking in a fish nearly as big as itself.

The way of a loon is wild and if you take one captive it will only die. Should you desire to capture any wild thing, in spite of a forbidding law, don't start on the loon—a bird only happy when swimming or diving in one of the cold lonely Canadian lakes.

Loons are not keen about people or civilization, as the head of Island Park had found. In fourteen years' residence across the Bay, Mr. Potter had met only one great northern diver. He took it to a pond, but it sulked and refused food—even a nice fillet of fish—and lived but two days. He had previously found one in a little ditch north of the city which had evidently strayed from its course. He carried it to the Riverdale zoo, but it also died.

It has always seemed to me that when birds become tame enough to eat out of your hand, they are hardly more glamorous than hens. Even as the swamp cardinal flower, when transplanted to a hothouse, is less lovely than a red geranium.

How would you like to try what might be called aquatic falconry, instead of fishing laboriously with hook, line and sinker? You could get some young double-crested cormorants and persuade them to do the fishing.

Japanese fishermen used to train cormorants for this purpose and worked them at night with flaming torches for lure. A Japanese angler could manipulate as many as ten birds at once, by means of collar-attached reins held in his left hand and untangled with his right. When all his flock had caught fish, the live "dip-nets" were pulled aboard a boat and forced to release the fish, after which they were urged to go down for more. They were fitted with ring or neck-strap loose enough to permit breathing, but so tight they couldn't gulp the fish.

In China, the cormorant has been domesticated for ages, raised from eggs hatched under hens. Fishermen went out with long, narrow boats, their gunwales lined with unleashed cormorants which they drove into schools of fish. Each bird knew what was expected of it—even its own "station" along the boat's gunwale where it perched erect until time to dive for a fish.

The European cormorant—rare now—was once used in England to catch fish for sport, and an American writer thought it would be feasible to train our double-crested variety "to fish for mankind, too."

Curator L. L. Snyder once reported a small colony of cormorants established on an island in Lake Ontario, off Prince Edward County. The curator calls this bird an "animated tripod," because of its peculiar stance—its two broad feet and long, stiff tail, which it uses as a prop, making a firm base. Unlike the goose, the cormorant's four toes are webbed.

They lift their feet high when they walk, in a most absurd fashion, whence may have come the "goose step." One of their names is "nigger goose," and they have been mistaken in flight for the Canada goose, though their dark coats, smaller size, longer tails—and silence in flight—should differentiate them.

The only time the cormorant finds his tongue is during courtship. He cries "Oak, oak, oak," a hundred times and more. A Cornell thesis writer says his love song resembles "the choking sensations made by a cat." Another pen dubs it a "gargle-like croak."

Shag is another name for cormorant, of which my first glimpse was along the Gaspe coast, in flight. I thought it must be some kind of a black goose. It was too large for a duck, and its rapid wing-play and forward thrusting neck suggested a wild goose.

The double-crested cormorant is a controversial bird. Fishermen around the Gulf of St. Lawrence used to complain that the cormorants made serious inroads into the seafood fishes. But the Canadian Government investigated and "proved beyond doubt that their depredations were greatly overrated." They rarely eat fish palatable to man.

The last time I saw cormorants was also on the Gaspe coast, at Percé. Hundreds of these queer upright creatures were ranged in an even row along the entire top of Percé Rock, facing west, like a living fence in clear outline against the sky.

GULL

There is no memorial—yet—to the seagull in Canada. But over in Salt Lake City stands a marble shaft crowned by a ball supporting two marble gulls in the act of alighting. The monument was erected in 1858 by grateful pioneers of Utah whose first crops were in danger of being wiped out by hordes of devouring grasshoppers.

By a lucky timing, hundreds of hungry seagulls came swirling over the land borne on the wings of the prevailing west wind from the Pacific Ocean, and their sharp eyes sighted the limitless spread of food. With a wild clatter of quill and feather castanets, accompanied by clamorous cries, the ravenous birds descended on the fields and made a clean sweep of the invading insect hordes. Hence the monument in marble.

The seagull's skill as scavenger may be no less

important than his avidity in dealing with grass-hopper gangs. Harbourmasters have great respect for these gulls. Each bird is said to glean two pounds of refuse a day from the waters. Then consider the countless bays and small inlets (along our great lakes) that make perfect pockets for refuse—as well as safe harbours. The question pops up: What would happen if all the gulls in Ontario were to go on strike in their job of cleaning up these places?

Farmers of a later era have not all been as ready to raise shafts to gulls as were those Utah pioneers. One modern cultivator of crops in Rhode Island bought several tons of starfish to fertilize his fields, but was dilatory in applying the remedy to the land. He was unreasonably annoyed because (while putting on his delaying action) flocks of gulls discovered his mountain of smelly stuff and removed same in a quite un-Biblical way.

And gulls are clever. On a clam beach, note with what a high I.Q. the bird manages to get the shellfish out of its shell. It picks up a clam in its strong beak, flies up with it to a height of say thirty feet, drops it on a rock then descends to inspect result.

The shell should crack. But if not the gull goes up again and again with his precious morsel and keeps on climbing the air until the thing is conquered.

Actually authorities differ on the method adopted by gulls in picking up such things as shells from the beach. Some say feet. Some say beak.

In support of the beak theory is the fact that

gulls have an upper mandible that is ridged, and hooked at the tip and curved over the lower one, to facilitate no doubt the gripping of such prizes as the tournament golf ball which a gull once carried off (no penalty—it was ruled an act of God!).

Books call this the herring gull, though nearly everybody says seagull. It nests on the ground—on rocky or pebbled islands, often a mere bar of shingle thrown up from the lake or sea. The herring part of the gull's name comes from the bird's habit of scooping up small fry from beneath the surface of the water.

And it is probably its ability to digest almost as many kinds of food as a goat that enables it to subsist along the sea coasts from Alaska to the tip of South America, and from Greenland to the Mediterranean, as well as the inland seas such as our Great Lakes.

On the feudal Isle of Sark the law ordains that no seagull shall be killed, under penalty. The reason? Their cries as they circle the rocks serve to warn fishermen whenever fogs blanket the cliffs.

A great colony of terns—miniature gulls really—nest on Gull Bar, a tiny island out in Lake Ontario, two miles from the signal light at Point Traverse, southeast fingertip of Prince Edward County. There is a lively fishing settlement on the point. Fishermen have their own names for the birds. They call the common tern and the black tern—"white gannet" and "black gannet"—varying the former at times to "red shanks," because of its ruddy legs.

You pass Timber Island and the False Ducks to get to the bar—a mere acre of sun-bleached and surf-pounded pebbles that serves as nursery for the thousands of spotted eggs and mottled fledgelings found among the pebbles in July. The *Picton Gazette* records a visit there "under a lifting cloud of silver and black," as the screaming terns arose in sweeping flight formation when a disembarking "troop" of bird observers landed on their shingled sanctuary.

The *Gazette* refers to the bar as "a naturalist's paradise" and notes that the egg of an unusual migrant (the Caspian tern) was found there by the late Rev. C. J. Young of Toronto on June 6, 1917. Herring gulls winter on Gull Bar and terns occupy the place in summer.

The common tern lays its eggs on a gravelly beach where there is sufficient vegetation for a slight nest to hold the usual three eggs. On Gull Bar, shallow dents among the warm stones serve the purpose. If you put your ear to the ground you can hear the rustle of crackling shells as the fluffy balls emerge, helped in hatching by violet rays of the sun. Baby terns are brownish with brown eyes. The adult is pearl grey and silver with jet-black helmet, black-tipped wings, a coral beak and pink feet. Its forked tail and swift darting flight have won for the tern its other name of sea-swallow. (I hate to call this bird "common," though the books do.) This spear-winged beauty with dazzling white body, wings lightly washed with pearl grey, a velvet black, elongated cap, coral beak and coral feet, deserves a better fate.

The tern's flight is delightful. He has a forked tail to steer with. When we once made a quoted reference here to the tern as a "sea-swallow," a letter followed from Dick Bird, FZS, of Regina, who told us that in Southern Manitoba he had found these birds spoken of as swamp-swallows, adding that he thought "local names were always interesting."

At Centre Island one August day, a common tern flew in from the lake and circled for a while over the outer lagoon, just inside the breakwater. I was lucky enough to be at the beach while the bird put on a super show of fishing, with several successful strikes.

At a height of about fifty feet, it would hover (or stall) before each try. Then sharply turning its beak straight down as though pointing—or perhaps the better to sight a fish—the tern would fold its pointed wings and dive swift as a dart, cleaving the water without a splash, and coming up with a small silver shiner dripping from its bill.

It is one way a tern differs from the big gulls that sit jauntily on top of the waves and take what they can pick up—mostly dead fish. They do swoop down, at times, to gather food off the surface. But I've never seen a gull go right under water. Have you?

Of the fifty known varieties of terns in the world, the least tern (slightly smaller than the black tern) has been described as the daintiest of all seabirds. And of this littlest species Edward Howe Forbush tells the prettiest story. It appears in the new edition of *Birds of Eastern and Central North*

America by Forbush and May. . . . The great ornithologist died in 1929, but his bird stories will live.

In July, 1908, Forbush and a companion visited the Great Sands on the south shore of Martha's Vineyard, one of the few nurseries of the least tern then remaining in the northeastern United States. The story might be called "The Polite Male Tern."

The watchers heard a gentle twittering from a mother bird that nestled over a chick, and presently a male tern alighted at the nest bearing a tiny, bright silvery fish. Here let the fine Forbush pen take over:

Again the gentle twittering. . . . A little one stuck its head out from beneath the mother's wing, the father bird courteously passed the fish to the mother, and she fed the chick which begged with open mouth for it.

Again the provider winged his way over the sunny sea to return with another fish. The little ones were now asleep under the breast of the mother. He offered her the fish; she refused it. He flew away but soon alighted and politely proffered it again, only to be refused again.

At last, having full assurance that his family needed no more, he swallowed the fish himself.

And at the story's end Forbush puts the question: "Where shall we look to find a lovelier picture of happy, harmonious family relations than that shown here on this sandy beach beside the roaring surf?"

One of the most glorious of all seabirds is the gannet. The great white bird, with wingspread of six feet, looks like a figure out of mythology—Icarus with wings of wax—and few writers make use of its other name—the Solan goose. It is about

GANNET

a yard long, with strong wings and a powerful beak for catching—and holding—the small fry of the sea.

From a great height the gannet circles above the shoals. Then, partly closing its wings (and possibly its eyes), plunges down on its prey, and seldom misses. The plunge takes about fifteen seconds. The bird doesn't have to hold its nose when it dives, because of a structural peculiarity. Through evolution, no trace of a true nostril remains.

A brilliant pageant of snowy seabirds heading north above the storm-ridden Atlantic like white streamers being whipped along by a following gale, means spring on Canada's eastern seaboard.

For early in April the great migration gets under way when myriads of Canadian-born gannets that have wintered in the sunny south respond to a biological urge and begin their long wing-trek north again.

85

There is a continuous procession sometimes extending well into May and the first landing field is Bonaventure Island, a government sanctuary near Percé Rock, where thousands will drop out of the line to alight on old familiar ledges and take up claims to nesting sites. . . . Next stop is Bird Rock (off the Magdalens), then Anticosti Island, and at the top of the Gulf of St. Lawrence, Cape St. Mary, off Newfoundland.

Soon you may be able to see on the high shelves of Bonaventure Island, (if you travel that way) thousands of gannets with one chick to each mated pair, the parent birds taking turn in guarding the young until their wings are strong enough to venture out into the air by themselves and parachute down into the sea two hundred feet below.

It was my good fortune to visit there in September, 1934, one of a party of (lucky) thirteen, in a small fishing-smack piloted by a local celebrity and bird authority, Capt. William Duval who (we were told) was a great-great-grandson of a privateer, Peter John Duval, to whom King George III of England gave Bonaventure Island.

Capt. Duval spun us through a choppy sea to Bonaventure where he coasted as close to the cliffs as he dared, to give us the full thrill of gannets in flight, swirling overhead like alabaster fish in a giant glass bowl. . . . He pointed out a few kittiwakes, sea pigeons and comic puffins, that had stayed quietly on the lower ledges instead of joining the tempestuous wingcade.

Sirens have been taboo (boat sirens, of course) at Bonaventure since the island was declared a

CANADA GOOSE

sanctuary for seabirds by the Canadian Government a quarter century ago. Ships cruising along that stretch of the Gaspé coast are cautioned to withhold their whistles until well beyond earshot of the nesting birds.

For it was found that the nervous feathered folk (gannets in particular) when alarmed by the shrill blasts would scramble off the ledges in such haste that their eggs would frequently be rolled off into the Atlantic, and the lives of innumerable progeny snuffed out in consequence.

Gannets begin to trek south about September 20th, as soon as young are able to keep the pace. They first move out to the Grand Banks, partly to try young wings, also to feed on a fresh supply of fish to fit them for the long flight.

The honk of Canada geese in V-formation may be a sign of spring or a harbinger of winter. Noisy fliers, the only time this sagacious species ever flings caution to the winds, is in flight. They trust to their clipper wings to outdistance danger. Geese have been clocked at a mile a minute. When you see them riding the sky, they're sticking out their necks with a vengeance—not looking for trouble, but to avoid it.

Does a sudden massed retreat of wild geese from the Arctic regions signify the end of our Indian summer? I put the query to Prof. J. R. Dymond, then director of zoology, Royal Ontario Museum, whose smiling, laconic reply was that he didn't think the "wild things" were any wiser than we.

And why did they always say "wild geese," and not "wild ganders?" Weren't there just as many ganders? The professor's comment on this was to hand me a bird dictionary from the museum shelves, wherein to look up the word "goose." It was, of course, "anser" (Latin) and this recalled a story my father told of Sir John A. Macdonald (when a young barrister), whose retort to an opposing counsel was, "Oh, a fit answer for an anser!"

While on the wing, every bird in the flock serves term as flight leader. At mating time, when ground sites are chosen, the newlyweds step around gathering beaksful of dry grass or seaspin, the goose plucking down from her breast to fleeceline the nest.

Sometimes a pair will get "high hat" and zoom to some hawk's deserted shack up in a tree. Later the little shavers have an exciting time. Small yellow bills poke through brittling shells and five oval bodies are covered with golden fluff. Then parents push nestlings overboard and they bounce on the ground below. They have soft light bodies with no bones worth mentioning, and as they beat their little wings, like a toy windmill, when parachuting down, serious harm seldom results.

Then comes the trek to water—led by goose and

gander—and goslings are soon bobbing on the surface, like fishermen's corks, among the reed beds where they learn to feed. Wild goslings get their dinners by tipping forward—tails up—sliding slim long necks under the surface where they grub for soft gooey food. That's what makes 'em grow!

The nesting grounds of the blue goose had remained one of the elusive mysteries of bird life until the Canadian explorer-naturalist, J. Dewey Soper, acting under direction of the Department of the Interior, put a period to the long quest on June 26, 1929, when he discovered in the forlorn, fog-ridden, storm-swept lowlands of the Foxe basin coast of Baffin Island, countless numbers of nesting blues.

And it was "about the last place one would expect such prolific abundance," Mr. Soper said, since the nesting region presented, "superficially at least, a polar panorama of desolation; of vast, sodden marshlands bounded by reeking mudflats and everlasting ice; of a gloomy land haunted by leaden skies and harassed by chilling gales of rain and snow."

And in that sodden and undulating Arctic tundra in June was found a vast nursery for millions of tiny baby blues that looked utterly frail and helpless, yet were really tough and, it was said, could run like the dickens when only a day or two old!

Mr. Soper's discovery was unique (F. H. Kortright points out) in that it was no accident but the result of "a direct, intentional research." Mr. Kortright notes also, in his book *Ducks, Geese and*

89

Swans, that another breeding ground was located in 1930 on Southampton Island, several hundred miles west of Foxe basin, by George Miksch Sutton.

Soper, by the way, had a river in Baffin land named after him, while Sutton's name is perpetuated only in a warbler he discovered in West Virginia. . . . That's gratitude.

Lesser snow geese frequently travel with the blues. Blue geese come south in the fall by easy stages and in immense flocks, down the east coast of Hudson Bay to the south tip of James Bay where they make their first long stop to feed and gabble and gossip. Their chatter sounds like an endless repetition of high-pitched ga-ga-ga-ga-ga-ga-ga.

The main flocks are said by various observers to fly nonstop from James Bay to their winter resort along the Louisiana coast. But I am certain that many slip away unobserved out of the Cook's tours of the skies and drop down in Southern Ontario to see for themselves other points of interest such as our nice marshes around Toronto and the Jack Miner ponds at Kingsville.

Herbert K. Job, economic ornithologist, relates how he once built a blind at a certain spot along Louisiana Bay where thousands of wintering blue geese congregate at a gravel-spit (known locally as the "goose bank") to nibble the small gravel for digestive purposes. It helps grind their food and they are voracious feeders.

He wanted movies of the geese. And after waiting five days in dense fog and swarms of mosquitoes, with the characteristic patience associated with his name, Mr. Job was rewarded by what he termed one of the thrills of his life, when fully a thousand blues came, fed, and wallowed within six feet of his camera, entirely unsuspecting its blind potential.

Francis H. Kortright interprets the scientific name of snow goose as "from beyond the North wind." The greater snow goose, he states, is identical with the lesser snow goose, except for its larger size, and he quotes Audubon as saying that the first flocks to arrive at St. Joachim land there about September 12th and thereafter keep on coming in small flocks for about a month. Cap Tourmente is not far from St. Joachim, and there every fall, the "snowies" break their down flight to rest and feed after the long journey from their summer ground at the top of the Arctic, Ellesmere Island, 1,000 miles north of Foxe Basin, mentioned previously as chief nursery of the blue geese.

With bright sun shining on their alabaster wings and bodies, the snowies presented a magnificent pageant before taking off on the last lap of their journey south to winter.

One writer who immortalized this bird, was Paul Gallico in his imaginative book, *The Snow Goose*.

When ladies of a past era clamoured for swansdown to satisfy an aesthetic sense, they did not know they were helping to exterminate one of the most majestic creatures in the heavens—the trumpeter swan, an enormous white bird with wing-span of eight to ten feet.

BLACK SWANS

The trumpeter is rare now, and breeds in the wilder parts of Northwest Canada where its shrinking squadrons speed every spring in search of safer places to nest and bring up their downy young. These splendid migrants sweep past at such a great height when piloting their progeny south in the fall, we rarely sight their silvery wings, unless lucky as to the time, the place—and the field glasses.

Five trumpeter swans from British Columbia were presented to Princess Elizabeth while she and Prince Philip were on the Royal journey through Canada. But as the big white birds were flown over their heads (by plane direct to the Severn Wildfowl Trust in England), Elizabeth did not actually see her feathered gift until some weeks after she became Queen.

As Peter Scott, D.F.C., is honorary director of the Severn Trust, we wrote to him for news of the swans, and asked if the Queen (or her children) had seen them.

"We were of course delighted with the trumpeter swans," Peter Scott said in his reply. And he told of "their capture at Lonesome Lake, a small body of water among forested mountains in North-western British Columbia where the swans were cared for by a resident trapper, Ralph Edwards, employed as guardian, and whose young daughter, Trudy Edwards, looked after their actual feeding."

When securing the swans for the Royal visitors, Trudy was the one who led them into captivity, since the birds were familiar with her. She managed to decoy seven cygnets and one adult trumpeter into the trap. . . . But as the trap door was closing, the adult and two of the cygnets became alarmed and made a dash for liberty.

And so it was five (and not six as had been stated in the news item) that were finally flown to Vancouver and thence to Dorval Airport, Montreal, where they were "received" by William Taylor and R. D. Harris of the Canadian Wildlife Service, who fed and otherwise looked after them. Then they were shipped, by air, at midnight, February 11, 1953, en route to England.

"The swans arrived here on February 13th," Mr. Scott related, "and were released immediately in one of our large enclosures. They settled down remarkably quickly and after a few days were tame enough to come up and feed with other birds.

"We were lucky enough," the letter goes on, "to have a visit from the Queen and the Duke of Edinburgh when they were staying in the neighbourhood. She was very much pleased with her swans and indeed took a great interest in all she saw."

Canada's princely gift to the Royal couple should help materially in the preservation of the race of trumpeter swans.

The mute swan is also white but smaller—the one you see on ponds in High Park and at Toronto Island, and the kind mentioned, in *Young Lady Randolph*, as actually furnishing a fantastic centre-piece for the long oval table at Delmonico's in New York, where a banquet was given (in 1866) by Leonard Jerome to launch into society his brilliant young daughter, Jennie Jerome, who later became the mother of Winston Churchill.

Weeks of elaborate preparation preceded this coming-out party for the debutante. Mr. Jerome was determined that New York society "must receive Jennie as a princess." And it did, according to Rene Kraus in his fascinating book, *Young Lady Randolph*.

The banquet proved a sort of swan-song before Jennie went abroad (with her mother and sister), where she made further conquests including the important one of Randolph Churchill, the stormy petrel of English politics whom she married.

The banquet table was covered with flowers, excepting for the "ingenious device" in the centre, a pond thirty feet in length enclosed by a golden network from table to ceiling, like a tremendous cage, with its four superb swans brought from Prospect Park.

The only disturbance during the banquet was when a "fierce combat" took place between two of the swans, but it was of short duration. Above the table hung little golden cages "with fine songsters that filled the room with their melody." While around the board sat "the most beautiful flowers of

94

American womanhood, interspersed with the most eligible young men."

One place at the host's right was left empty until the company had assembled and the guests were "discreetly asked" to hold everything until the party was complete. Exactly timing her entry, Jennie appeared, frocked in white in contrast to her dark glowing eyes and dark hair, a radiant figure. Then glasses were lifted filled with "the incomparable '48 claret." Jennie was launched on the social sea "and floated away on her own power," like the swans on the central pond.

This story was recalled after reading the news item from London the other day that a bird house was being set up in Berkeley Square in which live British and Japanese nightingales were to "move in" for the Coronation and (maybe) sing.

In England, the mute swan was once regarded as the Royal bird, and required to have a registered mark on its bill. But by the days of Queen Elizabeth (the First) there were some 900 different swan-marks in the land.

The bird was featured in ancient legends, notably that of Lohengrin, the Teutonic knight errant who travelled the waterways in a boat drawn by a swan.

These mutes usually nest on small islands, and I witnessed once this delightful drama of a pair of mute swans at Catfish Pond in High Park. I recall the first scene as of a certain May 3rd, though swans were not the real purpose of the expedition.

I had gone out in the hope of seeing, once again, the rare king rail. For it was there on Sunday,

May 7, 1950, I had first seen one emerging from reeds at the edge of a small island at the southwest curve of the pond. An exciting event, because this largest species of rail had not previously been recorded in Toronto.

But this year, instead of a king rail, I noticed what looked like a large piece of white crumpled paper, through the then leafless shrubbery on the island, above the reeds.

Turning on my field-glasses, I saw it was not paper but a heap of white feathers, though so still that I took it to be a dead swan with long neck stretched to its full length, stiff on the ground.

Then a live swan came in sight around the island, swimming, and it began to patrol the pond back and forth close to the shore, unwilling (as I thought) to leave its dead mate. . . . But I guessed wrong, for the white shape sprang suddenly to life. Up came the head and limber neck and the bird began to preen her feathers. She appeared to be on a very rudimentary nest, a mere dent in the grass, and incubating eggs, of course.

The water patrol continued, for there were nuisance waterfowl in the offing. And during the hour that I watched, from the path outside the enclosure, the male swan chased away from his island (claim to which he had previously staked) at least a dozen mallard ducks and drakes who had dared to trespass on swan territory.

Mr. Swan wrathfully attacked one duck who seemed bent on making herself a nest in the reeds much too near his incubating mate. He took after her, darting out his long neck, after the manner of a great blue heron about to spear a shiner, and grabbed the duck's tail and shook her (seven times, I counted) until she quacked for mercy and when released, skittered off, half flying and half swimming, to a far end of the pond.

I went out to the park again, each weekend during May, and found the male swan still chasing mallards from his island home. And I wondered how long this performance would continue. What was happening to the eggs—why didn't they hatch?

On Sunday, June 1st, I went out to Catfish Pond again. There on king rail island we saw the male swan climb out of the water and approach his mate who was fondling some little balls of tawny swansdown.

Satisfied the drama was proceeding according to plan, we went further into the park to watch for awhile the elk and water buffalo. Then on our way back we spied at the west end of Catfish Pond the pair of mute swans swimming along, convoy style, guarding five small cygnets who were using their tiny black paddles efficiently.

And it was funny to see one wee cygnet climb out onto mother's broad back, cling for half a minute, then flop back into the water and proceed under its own steam.

Black swans have a history. Naturalists had thought the very idea of a black swan absurd— impossible! Swans had always been white. So what? A pair of blacks was found on January 6, 1697, by De Vlaming, a Dutch navigator, on a river in West Australia which was called, in consequence, Swan River. That thriving colony later adopted the black swan as its armourial symbol.

De Vlaming captured several before leaving Australia, and took one pair, alive, to Batavia, Java. Subsequent voyageurs—Cook and others—found black swans ranging all over the colony, and carried off specimens whose descendants are scattered widely today.

Those in our picture could trace their ancestry to Swan River.

One spring a pair of black swans nested near Toronto. I was walking past the pond, when a loud insistent call from a swan's horn arrested me, and I saw on top of a tiny shrub-covered island, a male obviously setting on eggs. He repeatedly megaphoned his mate, who was swimming leisurely around their island fortress, to come quick and take her turn at the job.

Obediently she clambered up the island to his side, and after waiting a minute—and her partner made no move to leave his post—she gave him an impatient poke with her coral beak. "You shouted for me. Why don't you go?" she clearly indicated.

He croaked his explanation, that she must dry off her feather coat, first, so as not to chill the eggs. And she proceeded dutifully, to perform this rite with her bill. Then he went for a paddle while his mate took over. A highly domestic drama.

But as to the pair in this picture, the affair is platonic, the swans merely swimming companions. They have been sailing about the pond for two summers without nesting. The male (in foreground) lost his mate three years ago, and you can see he still looks forlorn, and refuses to be consoled by another. Swans are said to be models of fidelity. They mate for life. They are also supposed to sing exultantly as death approaches. Wonder if that first dark lady sang to her mate at Centre Island before leaving him bereft.

My first sight of whistling swans was at midday on May 23, 1940, while standing on the corner of College and Yonge Streets. Three of these breathless beauties flew in a northeasterly direction, about 300 feet up, splendid in the sunlight against a blue sky, their long pencil-slim necks and their slow flapping wings distinguishing features.

This species is far from extinct, for it has long been rigidly protected, and still is, over the whole range of North America. Winters chiefly from Chesapeake Bay to North Carolina. When migrating north in spring, swans bottleneck at Niagara, where many meet disaster by being drawn over the Falls.

The legend of the swan song is laughed at as a myth by the more sophisticated ornithologists. But Mr. Kortright has quoted Dr. D. G. Elliot as having heard the real thing.

It was at Currituck Sound in 1898, when a swan mortally wounded in the air set its white wings and sailed slowly down, piping its death song while descending, and sustaining the melody until it reached the water nearly half a mile away.

The song was unlike any other swan note Dr. Elliot had ever heard—plaintive and musical, sounding at times like the delicate running of an octave. It was a song to remember.

5. Birds that Ride the Wind

Eagles, Vultures, Duck Hawks, Falcons,
Goshawks, Red-Tailed Hawks, Marsh Hawks,
Ospreys, Broad Winged Hawks, Pigeon Hawks,
Sparrow Hawks, Nighthawks, Swifts

TOM HOOD, THE POET, was off the beam when he said there was nothing nice in November—"No sun—no moon . . . no shade, no shine, no butterflies, no bees . . . no birds." There have been flocks of birds and butterflies and bees in Ontario in November and many moonlit nights!

Looking back on past Novembers, there was that very special Sunday when a birding companion and I were given the keys to an enchanted place out Bayview way, by Mr. and Mrs. James R. Mackintosh, ardent birders, while they went jaunting away to fresh fields for the day.

It was Indian summer weather. There were not only yellow jackets and wild bees and a few bumbles buzzing around, but here and there butterflies floated in the sunshine—mourning cloaks, monarchs, an orange sulphur or two and at least one wandering comma.

At noon, while at our picnic lunch on a warm, dry bank along the Don where it narrowed and wound glinting among tall elms and Corot-like willows, we scanned the sky wishfully and were suddenly granted the sight of a great dark bird which circled and sailed about 500 feet above us. Its wide wings swept the dazzling blue wall of the sky like a moving mural—startling when it swung about and the marble-white head proclaimed it a bald eagle. . . . Then in less than five minutes a marsh hawk sailed into view from the east at about the same height. They swirled in companionable circles for a few minutes and the sky seemed very empty after they had gone.

"Dignity, elevation, repose are his."

The words are John Burroughs', the great naturalist of an earlier day, and his reference was to the bald eagle. Mr. Burroughs should have added, "Sometimes."

For, as in the case of a mosquito and a man, the dignity and repose of many a mighty eagle has been shattered, it seems, by the tiniest of feathered creatures—the hummingbird. Confirmation came for me in a drawing I saw by Harrison Weir (English artist in the 1850's) showing a ruby-throat clinging to the head of an eagle in flight. The text stated the hummer was pecking out eagle feathers and scattering them in a stream behind "the tortured bird" as it dashed screaming through the air "in the vain hope of shaking off its puny foe."

Hardly less strange was the close view I had of a big crow being beaten to the ground at Toronto Island by a kingbird. When the crow picked itself up and flew off several feathers were plainly missing.

The English naturalist whose book Mr. Weir was illustrating remarked that, though the eagle was "king of birds," he was often pestered by such tiny adversaries as the humming bird. The author stated a curious fact: Seldom more than two eggs were laid by an eagle. But if three were laid, two proved females. Thus one became an "odd bird" who never found a mate—grew to be outsize and ferocious, ranging the hills and crags, a terror to every other bird and beast encountered.

Many countries have set the eagle on a pinnacle. Romans named him "Bird of Jupiter." He streaked across the skies trailing thunderbolts. Our Red Indians revered him for his courage, strength and fierceness. Chiefs, endowed with these qualities, were permitted to adorn their heads with eagle feathers, each plume signifying an enemy slain. When the slain were numerous, the headdress would sweep from crown of head to foot of robe in a cascade of quills.

Eagle feathers were worn by Scottish chieftains in their bonnets to signify rank. Three feathers marked the chief. His son was permitted only two.

The name bald eagle is a misnomer. He needs no restorative for his densely feathered hood like a judge's wig. Early naturalists may have confused him with the bare-headed vulture to which he is akin. His range extends to Northern Quebec and Yukon, where a larger type is found. Male and female adults have white head and white tail. Young bald eagles take three years to show white feathers. Average weight of full-grown bird is twelve pounds. Wingspread from six and a half to eight feet. It feeds largely on fish, and when ice comes between eagle and finny prey, it consoles itself with fat rabbits, squirrels, mice and snakes.

From Mrs. S. Alfred Jones, Victoria, B.C., came word of a lone eagle with a huge wingspread that had fooled spectators at an air show at Cassidy Airport, near Nanaimo.

As is known, eagles while soaring and gliding keep their wings at the horizontal, and until this particular eagle broke from soaring to flapping, onlookers took it to be one of the exhibiting planes. It was definitely intruding in airport territory!

A radio voice told one night of excited bird enthusiasts having watched a lone eagle perched on an icefloe in the upper Niagara River, heading swiftly for disaster, until within 300 feet of the falls, when the great bird safely took wing. It was reported to be a golden eagle from Navy Island.

It is possible that a young bald eagle, as frequently happens, was mistaken for the golden eagle, which P. A. Taverner claims is "a rare sight in Canada except in the mountains of British Columbia." And he points out that "the majority of popular reports of this species are based on the juvenile bald eagle."

These incidents recall an experience my late sister (Helen Egerton) had—in the fall of 1949, I think it was.

From an east window of the Egerton's house in Toronto, Helen was watching what she thought was a large plane heading west. When suddenly the wings broke from glide to a flap, and she was thrilled to discover it was a great eagle.

Next morning *The Globe and Mail* carried confirmation in a news item about a golden eagle reported by more than one birdwatcher who had sighted the big feathered plane soaring over Toronto.

A proverb in Jewish literature asserts that a vulture in Babylon could spot a carcass in Palestine. As Babylon—they say—was more than 600 miles from Palestine, that must have been a remarkable feat.

The one we are most apt to see in Canada, the turkey vulture, is two and a half feet long, with a wingspread of six feet. Its eggs are white with lilac and brown spots; one would make an omelet.

Though its food is mainly carrion, a vulture will eat snakes, toads, and rats if handy. It does not attack chickens or game birds, preferring to pick on dead ones. Elongated beak is sharply curved at end. Reddish head and neck are bald, with wrinkled skin, hence its Christian name of "Turkey." Wings so long that, when walking, bird keeps them semi-extended, so as not to wear off the edges on the rocks. When folded, they extend beyond the tail.

An English writer (in 1856) dubbed the vulture "a pseudo-British bird" and objected to its being catalogued with respectable birds. He argued that a vulture had no more right to be called English, because it was sometimes seen on the English coast, "than a daw to be reckoned as religious because (to borrow Hood's simile) it keeps a-cawing from the steeple."

He swallowed his prejudice to admire its marvellous flight and magnificent spread of wing.

Said it was "extraordinary" to watch it rise and "deliberately stretch out its wings to their utmost limit—an analogous action to yawning."

Aided by these enormous wings, the vulture floats in the air, without apparent effort, and stays up hour after hour with scarcely a flap, even to alter its course or to rise higher en route to the stratosphere. Centuries before man figured it out, vultures were taking advantage of favourable wind currents and avoiding the unfavourable ones. Or so the scientists say.

A great game with hawks is to try to tell them apart in the sky—rather than tear them apart with shot. And it's smarter.

Curator L. L. Snyder once told me that hawks were among the most difficult birds to identify on the wing. Looking up from the ground at the red-shouldered hawk as it soars into the blue (or grey) you see a big brown bird about the size of a crow, with broad expanding wings, a short square tail spread fanlike, with dark horizontal bands. The underwings and body appear dark, except for two translucent patches—one on each wing at the base of the primaries, somewhat like the "shothole" in a nighthawk's wing. These make a good field mark or (more correctly) a sky-mark, for red shoulder.

Scientists assert that birds are but "glorified reptiles." If this be true, it's dog eat dog, for red shoulder is a hearty consumer of snakes. His call is a piercing whistle, "Kee-yer!" with falling inflection. Smart bluejays often imitate their cry—to scare other birds, perhaps.

The duck hawk, or to give its romantic name, "Peregrine Falcon," is the largest of the falcon family. Others are the pigeon hawk and the small sparrow hawk. The duck hawk usually places its nest on some "inaccessible cliff," say the books. When attacking its prey, the peregrine drops with a wild rush and seldom misses.

Falconry, a 4,000-year-old sport that had its origin in Central Asia where it still thrives, is "as dead as the Dodo" in Canada, according to Claude May of Toronto who a decade ago had quite a lot of fun training a young duck hawk to be a good falcon.

But Mr. May admits having made a serious slip in his first attempt.

He had read "every blinking book" he could lay his hands on, he recalled, and presumably learned the one essential thing: that the falconer should fly the birds free only when they were hungry, so that they would immediately streak for the lure on hearing their master's voice—his whistle.

"But I thought those writers were a lot of old fuddy duddies," laughed the now mature falconer. "That's where I made my mistake. I fed my first young falcon right up to the hilt and let her go. . . . And that's the last I ever saw of her. She flew away with the hood, the bell 'n' everything."

The falcon by the way is a lady. The male, a third smaller and not so deadly, is known as Tiercel. The duck hawk is a counterpart of the noble peregrine falcon of Europe.

If you intend to capture a hawk with the idea of training for falconry, or even just keeping it for a pet, you better be careful how you treat the bird—if you listen to Mr. May. He advises that young enthusiasts should not attempt to train one in a city. It's not only hard on the bird but on the neighbours. Falconry is definitely a country job.

First step is "manning" the bird, i.e., carrying it around for hours every day and talking to it all the time, getting it used to your voice. Also petting it.

"But remember," you are warned, "petting doesn't mean what you think—stroking its head as you would a dog. . . . No nonsense like that! Hawks don't like you to touch their feathers. Hurts their dignity."

You'd never guess that petting, in falcon parlance, means: "A gentle stroking of the bird's feet."

The business of feeding is important. . . . Never give a hawk (or owl) straight meat alone. It needs roughage, and that doesn't mean bran. Meat should be mixed with a few feathers, bits of fur, and some short pieces of string. Replace some of the feathers or fur the bird would naturally get in its native wild life.

In its digestive process these separate from the edible meat and form into pellets which the bird ejects from its mouth each morning, politely called regurgitating. And by the state of the discarded pellet the condition of your captive can be determined.

Teaching the hawk to respond to the lure is something special. Mr. May used an old leather glove stuffed and with a pair of pigeon wings sewn on back. Realistic! . . . This he would swing from a leash while he whistled. Bird soon learns to associate the lure and whistle with food. Sort of "Come to the cookhouse door!"

A small metal bell is tied to the falcon's leg above the jess strap, so that when the falcon has gone down in cover (tall grass and such) while working over its prey, the trainer can locate him by sound of the bell.

Queried as to why and when he first took up falconry, Mr. May recalled that about 1937 Don MacKinnon had been the one who stirred his interest and taught him a lot. Any one familiar with falconry here would know of Mr. MacKinnon's prowess in the art.

Did Mr. May think the rumour true that the falconer was to blame for the reported decrease in our duck hawk population?

Certainly not in Canada, came the emphatic reply. There never had been enough of the sport practised here to have any effect on their numbers.

Curator L. L. Snyder once gave me a similar answer. Mr. Snyder said the few birds taken out of the running were inconsequential. And, on the contrary, falconry, he thought, would stimulate interest in birds in general. "It's a bird-hunter, quite true. But aren't we all?"

Mr. May added that "the undoing of the duck hawk was not the falconer—never has been. But in my opinion this hawk has had its greatest persecution from the boy with his deadly little .22."

The gyrfalcon inhabits the far north. Is seldom seen near settlements excepting on rare occasions during migration. It is one of the gallant company most highly esteemed by falconers of old and grouped, by early scientists like Cuvier, among the "noble" birds of prey.

Cuvier spells it "gerfalcon." I found this in his valuable work, *The Animal Kingdom*, which Mrs. J. K. Hill (Island of Orleans) very kindly contributed to my shelf of reference books. Among the Ignobles, Cuvier lists the goshawk, Cooper's hawk and the sharp-shinned, that seem to kill for the sheer lust of killing.

Last fall, H. T. Trevanna of St. Catharines, whose drawings illustrate this book, and who has closely studied birds as well as art, endeavoured to identify a large bird with graceful flight, definitely a falcon. He described it as isolationist and a routine bird, since it was always alone, and passed over the same course each evening before sunset.

One evening he stood facing the east when there came in view a flock of red-winged blackbirds, "at first in open formation, but suddenly closed, and then bunched."

In a flash his mind bridged sixty years, Mr. Trevanna recalls, when as a boy in England he stood in a meadow watching a gathering of peewits (lapwings), whose formations and manoeuvres fascinated him as they "wrote their message in the sky." Other flocks appeared and "joined in the display, until they became a vast assembly. Then, in an array of winged discipline, they gathered their forces and swept onward." The sight always stirred in him "a feeling of utter desolation," he tells.

That mental picture vanished, and he was back in St. Catharines gazing skyward, when the big bird he had been trying to specify, "deviated from its customary course as it came down from the north, and headed straight into the oncoming flock of blackbirds. And so swiftly that the wing movement was scarcely discernible and the space between the attacker and the flock was eliminated with the action and speed of a zipper."

The flock split asunder, "and bounced in the air as if actuated by an invisible juggler." And out of this confusion emerged the falcon with a captive. The flock rapidly reformed and disappeared. All but one which Mr. Trevanna thought was the captive's mate.

This valiant little fellow, the story goes, "was up and down on the head of the falcon until the two of them seemed to go plump into the treetops." Still watching where they disappeared, Mr. Trevanna exclaimed, "Well, bless my soul! Look what's coming." And out flew the brave small bird, still alive, and gaining altitude, in spite of bedraggled feathers.

Hundreds of little birds, in hiding, must have witnessed that scene of courage, the watcher felt. For he distinctly heard sparrows that had taken shelter under his awning, chatter approvingly, as the bedraggled hero flew past. "My heart also went out to him. It was good medicine," he said.

On the other hand, he has great admiration for the gyrfalcon, "fearless and gallant, and not cruel—taking toll only when in need of food."

The last he saw of it was when it dipped so low that he could plainly observe the shape of its head and its keen eyes. Then he felt sure of his bird.

A young goshawk that pounced upon and killed a five-pound White Sussex chicken, near Oriole Village north of Toronto ended its career ignobly in the refrigerator at the Royal Ontario Museum where Clark Locke—who shot the hawk—left it and where it tipped the curator's yardstick at twenty-three and a half inches, which is an inch or two longer than an adult male.

The goshawk's appearance in the Toronto area was "unprecedented," a museum official stated. They usually keep to the more northern forests. Hunger could have driven it down. A young goshawk is more daring than an old bird. "And this one returned to the kill, again and again," before Mr. Locke could get it, he said.

In Cuvier's *Animal Kingdom* published in 1834 I find the goshawk listed quaintly among "The Ignobles," in contradistinction to the "true falcons," regarded as "noble birds of prey."

A field-mark of the goshawk is that its legs are feathered to "well below the knee," as Mr. Locke found on the bird he shot. The adult has a blue-grey coat, long, horizontally banded tail, white streak above the eye which is fiery red, and fierce enough to scare the least timid hen.

The juveniles have wavily-lined brownish plumage. And because of a marked likeness to the harmless red-tailed hawk, the latter is often blamed for the alleged misdeeds of the former.

J. J. Hickey, author of *Bird Watching*, mentions the red-tailed hawk by name when he says that "In the middle west, which some like to regard as the enlightened centre of America, red-tailed hawks are shot on sight." The species is commonly known as "hen hawk"—because it once got a hen!

A high authority on the food of hawks declares the nickname has put this handsome red-tail on the spot, so that the farmers regard it, generally, with suspicion and shoot it whenever possible. But the hen hawk should be protected, seeing that fully sixty-six per cent of its food is injurious rodents, and not more than seven per cent poultry and wild game—these probably decrepit members of a tame flock, or crippled game birds. It also consumes pecks of grasshoppers—in season.

Well—shouldn't this fellow be allowed a chicken or two as a slight reward for his destruction of field mice, wood rats and rabbits?

And what a beautiful sight to watch him as he spirals up into the blue! As Thoreau once said— It was easy to buy eggs, but not to buy hen hawks, and the philosopher of Walden Pond deplored the fact that his neighbours would not hesitate to shoot the last pair in the country "to save a few of their chickens"—which economy he called "narrow and grovelling." He would rather never taste chicken, nor hens' eggs, than "never to see a hawk sailing through the upper air again."

To identify an adult hen hawk in the field, look for the bright, rust-red tail with brown band at square tip, edged with white. The hawk is dark brown above with mottled patches of grey and white. The underparts are creamy, with black chain-patterns along flanks. Beak a dusky horn colour, yellow legs and feet, and brown eyes. Its length from twenty to twenty-five inches. Young hawk's tail in first autumn, is not red, but brown with black bars. Its bills and eyes are yellow.

Like all hawks, except the nighthawks, the red-tails migrate by day. They fly south from about the end of October to November 12th. Some cross via Point Pelee, the most southerly point of Canada. And great concentrations are seen streaming over Hawk Mountain in Pennsylvania—now a sanctuary where thrilled birders watch from favoured ridges, once held by avid gunners who boasted the number of birds they could bring tumbling to earth.

Since the senseless slaughter has been stopped by conservationists (led by a Mrs. Edge, who bought the whole mountain) magnificent flight lines may be seen from the Mount Tom range in Western Massachusetts, well into Eastern Pennsylvania. These lines comprise several varieties of hawks—including the red-tail, whose flight numbers have registered as many as 6,000 in a single day.

The marsh hawk, or harrier, of light slender build with long wings and long tail, patrols marsh and meadow-land for field-mice, frogs and snakes. The ends of the wings look very like hands with pointed and darkened finger-tips.

The adult male is nicely ribbed and mottled and has the slate-blue back resembling the colours of a gull. A showy white patch between wings is visible

113

when the bird banks. White lines above and below yellow eyes look owlish. This hawk has not the reputation, attached to certain species, of frightening young birds. Fledgelings do not have to be warned to "duck" when gentle harriers fly back and forth, ever so low, over the meadows. They are out to rid the land of vermin.

While quartering the marsh, with the precision of a trained pointer, the hawk finds it easy to spot a frog. When courting, the male turns mad somersaults in the air to impress the lady, who gives no sign. Though thrilled, she's coy.

Marsh hawks are very valiant in defence of their young. Forbush describes their nest of dried marsh grass as neatly constructed, but with the damaging admission, "for a hawk."

The osprey, or fishhawk is a handsome, dashing bird of prey which as its secondary name suggests eats mostly fish, though it will turn aside when in the mood, to snatch the odd frog or water snake. Or it will even go for eels if eels happen to be slithering around in its territorial waters.

Evidence of a fierce nature is shown not only in its wild orange eyes, but in those scaly feet whose long strong talons are sharply curved like a cluster of steel fishhooks and capable of a deadly grip. . . . The osprey uses its feet to capture prey, after the fashion of falcons, rather than its beak like kingfishers and seabirds.

For extra equipment there are short sharp spines on its footpads resembling a minute pineapple growth, which assist the osprey to hold the most slippery customer.

If that were not enough, the bird has a reversible outer toe that can be directed backward to form a complete clutch—and no holds barred.

But this strangle hold may seal the Osprey's doom. For when it stoops from a height of fifty feet or more and seizes a fish that proves too heavy to lift from the water there is danger of it being drawn under and drowned. . . . Such incidents have been recorded by ornithologists.

Because the osprey has never been known to include birds in its diet, man is not bent on its destruction. Yet those gunners who go trigger wild when they see anything that looks like a hawk, as well as collectors of the osprey's beautiful eggs, have decimated its numbers seriously in certain localities.

W. H. Hudson wrote of it as "one of those species that linger on the verge of extermination." And Capt. C. W. R. Knight, the widely travelled British naturalist, was so concerned about the osprey's fate in Scotland (where this magnificent bird had been extinct for twenty years) that he took over two pairs from Gardiner's Island (off Long Island, N.Y.) in an effort to reintroduce the species.

When in Toronto in 1948 with his performing Scottish Eagle (which he quaintly called Mr. Ramshaw) Capt. Knight told me that one pair of these transported ospreys had nested successfully in the previous summer—somewhere in the Highlands . . . he wouldn't say just where, as it was

BROAD-WINGED HAWK

kept a dark secret from possible gunners and collectors.

The Captain described the osprey as a streak of feathered lightning and referred to Gardiner's Island as one place that this species flourished, where the most famous colony in the world enjoyed primeval freedom.

October days are glorious days for hawk flights and you may still see small bands taking advantage of favouring winds (usually nor'westers) as well as "thermals," which John Kieran describes as rising currents of warmer air which give the birds a lift on their journey. He quotes Kipling's line, "The wild hawk to the wind-swept sky."

Yes, autumn is the very time of year to scan the sky, for it is then that hawks (and eagles, too), gather in flocks in the far north and travel south together. . . . In spring they are more likely to straggle north unnoticed.

My biggest hawk thrill happened in 1949, when I watched from a vantage point in Queen's Park hundreds of the broad-winged hawks and lesser varieties sweep down under the stress of a north-west wind on their fall migration to their winter quarters in South America. It was a bright, boisterous morning with white billowy, clouds sweeping down over the city from the north. A friend at court telephoned to say that hawks were going over the parliament buildings in large numbers, and in three sizes.

It was just the sort of day that hawks would pick to travel. Moreover, Toronto is one of the main flyways of the hawk tribe in migration, and flights of these captivating creatures may be expected up to about the end of October.

Hawks came streaming along from the south-east, sometimes singly, but oftener in twos, threes and fours. Five was the most I saw in a group, in three hours of watching. It was soon possible to identify the "three sizes" mentioned by the civil servant.

Largest was the broad-wing, magnificent in dark silhouette against the alabaster cloud-puffs.

The broad-winged hawk is said to be the most gentle of all the larger hawks, both in behaviour and voice. They do not scream. But their cry as they flap and sail through the air has been likened to an intensified call of the wood pewee, that small flycatcher one hears in plaintive repetition throughout September days.

And because their appetite craves mainly rodents, harmful insects, and an occasional entree of snake, high authorities insist the broad-wing should be protected.

The Cooper's hawk is large as a crow, but with long barred tail and a noticeably small head for such a large bird.

Then the smallest (sometimes mistaken for juveniles because of their diminutive size) were the savage little sharp-shins, a holy terror to the song birds.

Curator L. L. Snyder revealed an exciting bit anent the sharp-shinned hawk after I told him of having seen a great concentration of thrushes at Toronto Island on a previous day. The curator linked my piece of news with the flight of hawks. He said that sharp-shins definitely follow the thrushes during migration. . . . "Nice to have your food supply with you when you're travelling," he opined, "But how about the poor thrushes!"

Broad-winged hawks have a reputation for good behaviour. So it may be that the sharp-shins use this species as a shield of respectability by travelling in their company, hoping thus to escape censure for their own misdeeds.

A pigeon hawk, or blue bullet, as it is sometimes called, was found in baggage room at Toronto Union Station one day and taken to Humane Society kennels. It is one of the "honourable" falcons, and in speed and drive has been likened to the peregrine, prince of the line, commonly known as duck hawk. And when Inspector Gordon Stamp took it out of the cage for me to inspect, he agreed that it had a fierce, wicked-looking eye. He was careful to arm himself with long thick leather gloves against the falcon's wickeder claws, remembering a few near scratches from a snowy owl he had once handled at the kennels. . . . The captive gave a shrill cry not unlike that of the sparrow hawk.

Modishly matching its eyes, our captured falcon had jade green feet with sharply-curled black claws, and a green cera (or cere), the patch that covers the base of the beak through which nostrils are pierced. This was evidently an immature female about thirteen inches in length. The ladies are always larger (and, of course, deadlier) than the male. She was wearing a brownish cloak striped, rather than the gull-blue topcoat affected by the male.

The pigeon hawk nests north to the tree limit, almost entirely in Canada, and is mainly seen in the Eastern United States during fall migration when it follows flights of smaller birds with variable success. It sometimes hangs about flocks of slow-flying blackbirds and "comes up with one in each fist," says an observer. Hundreds speed over Hawk Mountain.

Taverner, Canadian authority, claims that the pigeon hawk, with its sharp-pointed wings and toothed bill, probably once preyed on the passenger pigeon. Some say it looks like a pigeon. I could see no resemblance.

Frank and John Craighead, skilled southern falconers, who have flown almost every known species, place the pigeon hawk high on their honour-roll. . . . They fly their small hawks at

119

sparrows instead of larks, and use starlings as lures for the big falcons.

The brothers tell (*in National Geographic*) of a trip they once made to Canada on purpose to photograph the pigeon hawk, which they noted was "a northern bird and a late nester." One nest they took was just over the Canadian border.

They found these birds very pugnacious, and told how "the female struck us so often on the head as she flew past that we ducked unconsciously every few minutes while changing the films in our cameras."

The female usually fed the young, so the male had to transfer his prey to her. Once they saw the male return with a small bird which he transferred from his feet to beak, then perched on a spruce limb to await the female, who on hearing his call flew past and took the bird out of his beak with her feet, while flying.

Another time they watched a fine performance, with both birds in the air together. The female flew over the lake, at his call, and when her mate dropped a bird from above, she quickly turned over, in flight, caught the prey adroitly, and carried it off to the nest. . . . The pigeon hawk is a smart bird!

Dr. Oliver H. Hewitt, of Ottawa, told Toronto Field Naturalists once that if a farmer was menaced by meadow mice, "let him call in a pair of sparrow hawks" to patrol his fields. Each young hawk, he said, "requires about one meadow mouse a day." Hard on the mouse—yes! But mice are "hard on" the cherry trees, which they ruin by girdling. So it's tit for tat, and this merry little hawk should be protected.

Smallest and most beautiful falcon, hardly larger than a blue jay, the male has a chestnut back, bluish wings, a stand-up barred collar and barred tail. Stupidly named, for it neither looks like a sparrow, nor does it eat them—when it can get grasshoppers or mice!

Its flight has been called swallow-like, but that is only when the bird is not hunting food. Then it hovers, like a kingfisher, before plunging to the ground on its prey—grasshopper or mouse, dependent on the season. You may hear the hawk squeal like a mouse and wonder if it is thus trying to entice some meadow mouse into the open for an easier catch.

A playful fellow, it frequently teases flickers in its range, but flicker doesn't mind. In fact, it often abandons its own nesting cavity in an old orchard tree to the hawk for later comfortable occupation.

The southward flight of hawks continues till about the end of November, and in a mild season they may delay migration well into December. Sparrow hawks are generally among the late leavers.

This small hawk closely resembles the kestrel (or windhover) of the Old Country, and not the English sparrow hawk with which our sharp-shinned hawk is frequently confused.

A man once hailed me in the *Globe and Mail* elevator curious to know what were those birds

NIGHTHAWK

that "squawked" (in the sky) after all the other respectable birds had settled down in the trees for the night.

It could be the nighthawk. And when I described its manner of flight and its cry, he said, "Yes, that's it!"

It darts about the sky till long after dusk, in a curious sharp-wing flight, doing hairpin turns and scooping up mosquitoes or gnats in its cavernous, whiskered mouth. And if it dives near enough, you may see those white, round wing spots (called shot-holes), and hear the wind swish through its feathered rigging.

The scientific name for nighthawk is given as Chordeiles minor, prettily translated Harp of the Evening. But the classic ornithologist who wished that pretty name on a tough old bird must have drawn deep on his poetic license to suggest a harp—unless the sort kids mistakenly call "juice harp."

122

For that weird boom made by the wind in the wings of a nosediving nighthawk in June, always sounded (to me at least) like nothing more musical than the voices of over-sized sparrows, heard as they fly. Or like the slipping of a G. violin string.

One year, toward the end of August, I watched a flight of forty nighthawks playing about on the eve of departure. They circled and swirled against a curtain of storm clouds—their behaviour quite different from that in springtime. There was no screaming nor diving. They flew at a low level, and I could see their forked tails spread open, and snap shut, like a Victorian fan. They had a pretty trick of rapidly beating the wings, then gliding like small boys on a pond learning to skate.

Nighthawks migrate at night and feast at their usual time (twilight), descending to rest along woodsy hedges by day, flattened lengthwise on tree branch or fence-rail.

The tail is spiked like woodpecker—a fact seldom noted. The nighthawk is usually shown prone on limb with wings and tail folded. The spiked tail could act as a brace in assisting the bird to rise from the nest. Its feeble feet are no help. It is unable to take one step unaided, and cannot even perch.

Squirrel-like are its prominent eyes; and they're very revealing. Bird seems to sense this. So, when enemy approaches—down go the eye-shades! One September a belated nighthawk rested for an afternoon on the gable of a neighbour's attic roof. It may have missed the flight going south. It seemed tired. Its throat throbbed continually like pearly balloon beneath a tree-toad's mouth when it trills. It had a white clerical collar under its chin, and almost no beak.

If the nighthawk had sense of humour, it could laugh at birds that spend their labour days building nests, when all it has to do (without any preparation) is to lay two spotted eggs on bare ground, or rock, or upon the high pebbled roofs of town houses. The female does most of the incubating, and is marked like her mate.

Gunners who used to think it smart to wing a darting nighthawk, have changed their tactics. Brought to earth, they found these robin-sized birds mostly wing-bones and feathers.

So there's the nighthawk—innocent of all harm—and to be blessed for its destruction of mosquitoes.

Recently at Avenue Road and Bloor, I saw seven nighthawks within my range of vision, at the same time. Not easy to count these dashing birds. They went like the wind, sweeping across the heavens like dark meteors, covering an expanse of sky from Queen's Park north to Avenue Road, then west over Varsity Arena and on to the weather bureau and east to Bay and Bloor.

And if there were seven nighthawks in that small space, how many, think you, would there be, hawking mosquitoes over the entire ceiling of Toronto?

They seem most alert on a sultry evening when thunder storms are brewing in the smoky copper cauldron of the night. It is fascinating to watch their terrific speed. And I know of no other bird of its size that can stop so suddenly, or make such sharp, spectacular turns.

To the casual observer the chimney swift is regarded as a kind of swallow. Scientists say the resemblance is "merely superficial," and have grouped them with the whippoorwill, nighthawk and hummingbird. As swifts are in flight from dawn to dusk, their wings have gained length and strength at the expense of their legs and feet, which have become partially atrophied. They could neither walk nor perch if they were paid, but can cling to a rough surface. The hummer cannot walk, but it can perch. The nighthawk and the "whipp" are unable to perch. They have to lie lengthwise on a limb.

Baby swifts are a mass of spiney quills—not very comfortable for parent bird to sit on. Feathers sprout later, then the young climb out of nest and hang onto inside of wall, for a time, before trying their wings in the sky. Pitiful wails are heard inside the chimney, for the young swift has been called the cry-baby of the bird world.

John D. Carter of Landsowne, Pa., a retired research chemist whose "hobby is an interest in taxidermy and museum exhibition," reports that it has "only recently become known that the winter home of the swift was in the heavy forest along the eastern slope of the Andes Mountains in South America." Or, to be more explicit, in Eastern Peru.

This is interesting in the light of previous records. Taverner, in his *Birds of Canada* (1943), states that "the winter home of the chimney swift is unknown." And W. W. Cooke in an American monograph on migration, says: "A remarkable fact concerning the swift is that no one has yet discovered where it spends the five months between the time it disappears from the northern coast of the Gulf of Mexico in November until it returns in March." Thanks possibly to bird-banding, their winter resort is now no longer the swift's secret.

One reason we are slow to identify swifts is that they fly so high, in order to hunt an exalted type of gnat. They are rarely seen "hawking" on the swallow's low level, over ground or water. Like Virgil's bees, they only drink on the wing, and take a flying shower bath in the surface of pools. Gilbert White "never found any rivalry or hostility between swallows and swifts."

The swift could have been named for its speed, which has been likened to the rush of a meteor. Capable of 150 m.p.h., one species is said to touch 200. Unmeteorlike, they dash around in circles, especially before swirling down into their chimney dormitory at night. A field mark is the swift's narrow scythelike wings that extend beyond its square, spiked tail which acts as a prop, like the woodpecker's.

Edible swift—so-called because their nests, of a superior kind of white gelatinous substance, are good eating—inhabit the Malayan Isles, from where a large trade has been carried on, during centuries of culinary history, with the Chinese, for conversion into birdsnest soup.

6. "Look for Birds with Your Ears"

Wood Pewees, Kingbirds, Crested Flycatchers,
Chipping Sparrows, White-throated Sparrows,
Fox Sparrows, Whippoorwills, Goldfinches,
Wood Thrushes, Thrashers, Ovenbirds,
Mourning Doves

"LOOK FOR BIRDS with your ears," was a good piece
of Irish advice given to beginners in bird watching
by that great Canadian naturalist, W. E. Saunders.
And there is no better way than the Saunders' way
to find the little grey wood pewee.

Schuyler Mathews has credited this flycatcher
with operatic ability. He claims it repeats a frag-
ment from "Fra Diavolo." But to the uninitiated,
it simply calls "pee-a-wee! . . . pee-a-wee!" drawled
at intervals all afternoon, and varied only by an
occasional indolent ending, "pee-urr," on a falling
inflection. This is one of the loveliest voices of late
summer, and I have heard it to the end of September. He is difficult to see, for the pewee keeps
hiding in the top branches of trees.

A trifle smaller than the phoebe and larger than
the least flycatcher, the wood pewee sits bolt
upright on the branch as if lectured on posture.

WOOD PEWEE

Though it can unbend in a flash when a choice
robber-fly tries to pass, or a long-legged crane fly, or
a water strider. And it can swallow a wasp (sting
and all) without a quiver. The pewee has two distinct wing-bars, and does not wag its tail like the
phoebe.

Smallest of its kind, the least flycatcher has
other distinctive features besides a diminutive
stature. The olive coat has two white wing-bars; a
pale gold eye-ring accents the shining dark eyeball
that resembles a ripe choke-cherry.

One of his given names is che-bec, but ignoring
the book, when hunting flies in his favourite prov-
ince, the little fellow calls himself "Ke-bec!" and
in perfect French. This call-note, uttered with a
thoroughbred toss of mane and flick of tail, confirms the bird's identity.

While some birds like to lounge on a limb, this
prim little flycatcher sits very erect, when he

perches, with tail pointing straight down, suggesting a secondary name—the perpendicular bird—though he has to assume a horizontal pose when darting out after the odd fly.

A busy beeyard is a surprisingly good place for bird watching, as the quiet work of the beekeeper does not seem to alarm or scare the birds away.

The kingbird (or bee-eater) may swoop into a beeyard, snatch a drone and fly off with it for food.

Why the name kingbird? The obvious answer concerns the defined domain where he rules. His nest is his castle. But a subtler reason was given me at the Royal Ontario Museum by Curator L. L. Snyder. The male has a red-gold patch on top of his head which few ever see as it is hidden by a pompadour of black feathers. But when he feels the kingly urge (and if you happen to be one of the elect) the kingbird will part his crest for you. There's a dazzling glint, and he calls you to "Look, quick!" if you want to see his crown jewel. Imaginative writers have suggested the concealed crown is used as a decoy for bees which, in mistaking it for a marigold, get snapped up. The honey-man calls the kingbird "bee martin."

Though his preference is for wild bees, he does eat the occasional honey bee, but is smart enough (Taverner says) to pick on the stingless drone and not the bee with a dagger. So the apiarian should not worry.

What makes the crested flycatcher bristle and shout when defending his home and family in the stump? Courage! And he wouldn't be a cousin of the kingbird, who often plucks feathers from the hide of a marauding crow, if he hadn't courage.

About the size of a kingbird, the male has ornamental crossbars forming an attractive pattern on his olive-tinted coat. Underneath, he is a rich primrose. Chestnut wing and tail feathers are showy when fanned. The male's strident shout scares many a bigger bird, especially in the nesting season, when jays and starlings try to torment him. He routs them all.

Though once a forest bird, this feathered flytrap has made the best of things, since many old forests have gone by the board. Now it is frequently found nesting in gnarled old orchard trees or their equivalent—a holey stump—where it cheerfully moves in with its furniture after a woodpecker family has moved out.

The farmer should coax this winged exterminator onto his land, for it consumes the boll weevil— a destroyer of crops, and a beetle that flouts the much-touted DDT.

One alias of the crested flycatcher is "snakeskin bird," bestowed because of a habit of decorating the nest with the cast-off trappings of a reptile. Romantic writers have suggested that the bird uses a skin to frighten away its enemies. But realists laugh this off as illogical—arguing that, as the big flycatcher's chief enemies are hawks and owls (who eat live snakes) they would not be likely to shiver at sight of a dead one. Moreover, how would they "sight" what is usually buried, with the birds in a deep, dark hole?

My own guess is that the snakeskin is adopted somewhat like a family crest—or totem—as emblem of the tribe.

A bird watcher from Crystal Beach reported that a pair of crested flycatchers arrived in the family orchard one summer and built high up in a tree-hole. Aware of the "snakeskin" fable, he decided to investigate, after the young were hatched and out of the hole. And with the aid of a ladder, he transferred the nesting material, carefully, to a box for examination.

The snakeskin was there all right, "though not draped around the nest, to scare intruders"—as had been stated by romanticists—"but broken up into a dozen pieces, and used, apparently, as some other birds utilize bits of paper."

"It may be that certain birds find the snakeskin gruesome. . . . But it is good material and I would say that, in this locality, there would be hundreds of cast-off skins to every pair of fly-catchers. And these birds do have a flair for the unusual."

He concluded with the fact that, besides the snakeskin, he found two smooth round pebbles among the nesting material, and a little conical seashell that had been pilfered, probably, from a child's adjacent sandpile.

June brings the grand jubilate of bird song, but tinged with minor strains of tragedy. In the very early morning, wild beautiful music runs up and down the scale of expression from ecstasy to anxiety—the joy of feathered songsters dropping

131

swiftly to low tones of distress when some furry monster is discovered padding stealthily in the deep grass, ready to pounce upon any helpless little bird that may fall out of the nest.

Neither joyous nor tragic, but one of the hottest sounds of summer is the song of the chipping sparrow called song by courtesy though really more of a buzz. Might be mistaken for the sizzling recital of cicada—the insect.

A small slim sparrow is Mr. Chip, who likes ragweed seed and will snap up the odd honey bee— though it's usually a drone. He generally arrives after you have sown your grass seed. And he likes nothing better than picking it up the minute you put it down.

The juvenile chipper, has a striped head. The adult covers its stripes with a henna velvet hood, though it leaves one long black mark near the eye. It hops on the ground with mechanical movements like a toy bird, and its call sounds more like the buzz of a hot locust than a song. The chipping sparrow's nest is interwoven with a horsehair lining—or was in the days before horses were rationed.

One June day I watched an amusing play on the grassy ground, in which a pair of chipping sparrows were taking part. The henna-headed male grasped the mate's tail, with his beak, and gave her a vigorous shaking. (I almost expected to see the tail come off.) Then Mr. Chip let her go, after which she set to work gathering rootlets and other bits of nesting material and flew away into the bushes with her mouth full.

132

It looked as though Mrs. Chip had been refusing (or perhaps just slow) to help with the nest building. And he was going to show her!

Hayfever-ites should welcome the chips because of their work against ragweed. They also devour thousands of crab grass (or finger grass) seeds—the bane of any pear farmer.

Sparrows are more easily identified by ear than eye. Some people would trade them all for a song-sparrow singing in the tip of a tree, declaring his to be the loveliest voice of the year—while others claim the Canada whitethroat's silver whistle expresses all the witchery of our northern woods. But you have to be up there to catch its magic, for the singer only releases fragments of its full song during migration.

These white-throated sparrows come down from the northern woods in small migrating flocks and you may see them hopping about on the ground and scratching among the brown leaves with both feet, like the towhee. If the food happens to be weed seeds, just out of reach above the ground, it is fun to watch whitethroats leap up and snap the seeds, then back to earth with their catch—repeating the exercise over and over instead of trying to balance on a stalk while they eat.

The Canada bird has a compressed conical bill, clamped tight (when not eating or singing), as if holding a secret. Maybe it does. A flock could be mistaken for house sparrows, at first, until their behaviour is noted, and you see the red-brown wings, striped head with jaunty white plume over

WHIPPOORWILL

eye, and the white bib covering throat where the sweet silvery melody is coiled ready to spring.

To me the fox sparrow is the richest, rarest of them all, with voice of compelling sweetness.

One autumn day two very red-brown fox sparrows richly striped, with reddish tails and red patches on wings and cheek, were first arrivals in our garden. Never before had I seen them around town. Other years I went to a certain wild place at Ward's Island to find the fox sparrows beside a weedy pool. Their song is sweet as honey.

The whippoorwill is a difficult bird to see, for it keeps dark in daytime. You can hear it, though, from dusk till ten o'clock and, when the moon is full, it "whipps" all night. Its scientific name is literally "cave-mouth," which is rimmed with bristles to help rake in the beetles.

Ivy Maison of Ottawa, who spends the summer in a cabin at Gatineau Park, wrote me once of a whippoorwill, "who does not say what he's supposed to. . . . This one, at least, distinctly says pur-pul rig, pur-pul rig, pur-pul rig, when he stations himself outside my cabin. And I have been able to turn the beam of my flashlight on him

134

hardly five feet away. . . . As he calls, he ducks his head each time, on the 'pur' syllable, almost touching the ground. It's most amusing to watch him bobbing and calling."

Other writers besides Miss Maison have been unwilling to accept "whippoorwill" as the proper interpretation of this bird's song—if you can call its reiterated cry a song, of which Taverner once said that no sound in the Canadian woods was so "poetically mournful."

Away back in 1748 when the Swedish scientific explorer, Peter Kalm, came over to this continent and travelled from Delaware to Quebec and from New York to Niagara (which was then in the wilderness) he wrote about this fascinating night-bird and declared that, "accurately speaking," its notes should not be translated whip-poor-will, nor whipperiwill (the Swedish way), but rather whip-periwip.

Unlike the nighthawk, to which the whipp is closely related, this controversial bird is not a high-flyer, but gathers in its flying food of moths and June bugs during low flights near the ground. And because it is definitely nocturnal, few watchers are lucky enough to get a good look. And when it drifts southward, silently, in September, it could be mistaken for a nighthawk.

Like the bat and the owl, the whipp's flight is noiseless. And like the nighthawk, which it strongly resembles, it cannot properly perch with its small, feeble feet, but rests its body lengthwise along a branch or a rock or a roof.

But while its feet are weak its voice is not. . . . John Burroughs recorded that one April morning, between three and four o'clock, he heard a whip-poorwill repeat his phrase no less than a thousand and eighty-eight times without a pause, which was probably a moonlight night when they say the whipp never stops!

The bird has an expansive mouth and when it splits wide open to gather in the bugs, you'd think its eyeballs might drop out from the pressure. . . . Whiskers serve as a screen to help catch the night moths, winged ants and beetles.

Burroughs, who was a meticulous observer, noted that whipp would sometimes call fitfully in September, "but quickly check himself as if he knew it was out of season."

No nest is built, but two blunt speckled eggs are laid on a bed of dry leaves on the ground, by the bird whose plumage of mottled brown blends perfectly like the partridge's coat with its surroundings.

When the eggs break to release the tiny feathered young, Mother Whipp gets frantic at the approach of a human being. She not only goes through the broken-wing act, but implores by every other known gesture, that they take her—if they must—but please spare the babies!

The goldfinch is a late summer nester. It has been said that this merry little feathered carpenter (with a heart as well as coat of gold) intentionally delays its home building until suitable nesting material is available. Waits until the heads of thistledown are fully fluffed out so that their silken

136

threads may be woven into a lining for the cradle and made snug for the expected goldfinch babies.

Frequently the young are only half grown and but partially feathered by the middle of September when chilly winds do blow.

On a day late in August, while watching for a glimpse of the gallinule that was tantalizingly tick-tick-ing among the rushes of Grenadier marsh, a more musical sound came from another direction. And a pair of goldfinches flew out from the shrubbery near the stream that feeds the marsh, and ascended into the sky, high above the tall tree tops, on one of their courtship flights.

Around and 'round they circled in that peculiar scalloping way of the goldfinch. One of the few birds that sing on the wing, their golden voices were bubbling with sheer joy as they reiterated the familiar rollicking measure, "per-cheep-oree, per-cheep-oree," on each descending curve of their ecstatic flight.

Suddenly a hummingbird darted into the picture—flew up out of nowhere (that I could see) and chased one of the pair for a minute or two. Then it darted away, but soon returned and again gave chase. Whether the little intruder was just playfully teasing the honeymooners, or was really envious, I wouldn't know. But after two slight engagements, the hummer retired from view.

Early that spring I had recognized a small flock of goldfinches just arrived from a long flight. They nibbled hungrily at buds in the top of a high tree, then stopped to sing at intervals as if it were June.

Not yet in their vivid yellow and black livery they shone a bronzy green in the sunlight. When they flew away across the ravine in a looped flight, I knew them by their gay wing-call.

The goldfinch is the only small bird that seems to like winging in the wind. On stormy days I have watched a flock of these bright feather-weights not only sing but dance among the waving branches of the willow.

And I am wondering why some smart young ballerina could not be induced to go out and watch these birds and make up a dance to correspond. Dressed in bright yellow, with a black sequined calotte and sharp little wing-sleeves of glistening jet, she could call her creation the "Goldfinch Gavotte."

When vagrant gusts of autumn wind stir up small whirls of the leaves and send them scurrying across the road like flocks of little brown birds I am always struck again by the likeness of blown leaves to dancing birds.

In our own garden a musical accent vibrated through the fall colour theme. The voice was that of a wood thrush whose matchless cadence has been likened to certain phrases in Faust's impassioned appeal to Marguerite—in her garden: "Come to me! . . . I am here. . . . Come to me!"

The composer might have "lifted" this song direct from the throat of a brown thrush in the tree. And why not? For Gounod was known to be deeply aware of Nature and her wild notes.

At the edge of a deep, mysterious wood late one summer, a very feminine brown thrasher stood on a stump, ready to speak her mind, viewing in distress the wreck of a beautiful brush-heap wherein she and her mate nested earlier in the year and had brought up a family of three.

Thrashers sing high but build low—sometimes on the ground. During that July, one of the parent birds (the pair so alike I cannot say which) came daily to the lawn, leading three grownups into whose wide-open beaks it transferred small bundles of bugs and spiders. They were big as the parents except for short tails that would one day grow to be five inches long—nearly half the length of the bird itself.

The avian speech, from the stump, was a bitter attack on the queer race of beings the bird had found tearing down their happy shelter which they had planned to occupy again next spring. Two of the "beings" were digging in the treeless foreground, with curious metal implements, and starting foundations for a monstrous thing called by these weird creatures a house. Well, such was life, she supposed. And there was nothing the birds could do about it but to fly further north.

Thrashers have a curved beak, yellow eye with black centre, and creamy breast covered with heart-shaped spots. The shapely head, back, wings and tail are a bright tawny brown, very like the wood thrush in colour and decoration. But the thrush has a short tail and its eye is dark brown, with no distinct iris and pupil like the thrasher's.

If acquainted with the bird, you will have noted

its "pliant russet tail beat like a frantic flail"—this vigorous habit being given, by writers, as reason for the thrasher's family name. It is the only bird I have ever seen attack and drive away a fighting robin from the robin's own territory.

Peering into the aforesaid brush-heap one day in June, to get a close-up of the bird on its nest, the parent thrasher hopped off and faced me, ready to attack. It made a hissing sound and showed me—the intruder—an angry yellow eye. I withdrew!

My first sight of a brown thrasher was on Macaulay Hill at Picton when, as a child, I was being taught about birds by my father who knew them well. The beautiful wild thing was leaping about among the low bushes, and I thought it must be a flying squirrel—and said so—until it began to behave as no squirrel would. It sang. I've never forgotten my early lesson on the thrasher.

Its song resembles that of the catbird, though the thrasher's voice is loud and clear, also more emphatic. And it repeats each phrase, which the catbird does not bother to do.

The ovenbird looks like a thrush, but isn't. He has a tawny ridge of feathers on head, outlined with black stripes, and thrush-like spots on breast. Is one of the few birds that walk rather than hop. Its walk is precise and comic.

The shrill call-note, oft repeated, was interpreted by John Burroughs as "Teacher! Teacher!" It always seemed to me more like "Teeter! Teeter!" And that is just what the ovenbird does when it

MOURNING DOVE

goes tripping along, on its pretty pink feet, over crisp leaves on the forest floor, which is one reason it is grouped with the Wagtail order of birds.

Its glorious flight song, heard in June twilights, was pronounced by that beloved old naturalist to be as far above its common call as the sky rocket outshines a Lucifer match.

One year blue jays built—and occupied—a nest in a low, spreading branch of one of the large pines at "Broadlawns," Oakville, where they raised a foursome of cute, noisy young jays.

Next spring a pair of wandering mourning doves, while looking over the land for a suitable site, spied the blue jays' abandoned quarters. And, defying the poet's dictum that "there are no birds in last year's nests," decided there soon would be.

They took possession of the old premises, to be altered according to their specifications. All the doves did (so far as I could see from my window) was to tear out the lining the blue jays had woven, and toss it overboard upon the lawn. I was curious enough to go out and examine the lining which reached the ground intact in one circular piece shaped like a saucer. It was then I discovered that blue jays do use horsehair.

The mother dove laid two glossy white eggs (her quota) on the platform of last year's blue jay bungalow. Doves appear to prefer the open-pattern floor, affording more ventilation. The eggs were plainly visible through the lacework of loose twigs and looked dangerously placed as if they might fall through to the ground. But they never did, and two young mourners were learning to fly from limb to limb before the end of May.

The mourning dove is a gentle, graceful bird with small head and a longer tail than the pigeon. It takes its name from its plaintive call, Oh-woe-woe-woe, that Taverner says "has a peculiar quality like that produced by blowing softly into the neck of an empty bottle."

Unless familiar with the song pattern of birds, or at least know the tones of their voice, you are out of luck, especially while the trees are in full leaf. You may walk through a wooded ravine and hear songs that tantalize and lead you on. Yet you can't identify the singers that are hidden behind a dense screen. The time to learn bird songs is early in the year while the performers are visible on leafless platforms.

7. Birds that Brave the Snow

Blue Jays, Canada Jays, Shrikes, Chickadees,
Nuthatches, Juncos, Cardinals, Woodpeckers,
Owls

OCTOBER DAYS are full of fire and colour and beating wings. Birds by the hundreds are still travelling southward—some flying off by daylight and low enough to be seen, others winging away in the darkness and at a great height.

If you are in a quiet country place and listen, as you look up at the stars, you are likely to hear piping bird voices indicating their course through the sky. At the time of the hunter's moon, if you fix your field-glasses on the round bright coin, you might see against its burnished face the actual movement—the sharp black tracery of myriad wings as they wave along in the stream of migration that is flowing forever south. This is no fantastic picture. It has been recorded many times.

But all the birds do not desert us. Some, like the blue jays, may linger around all winter.

In the woods just now, and in the parks—especially where oaks grow—blue jays are shrilling at the top of their voices as they gather acorns which they hurry to bury in the ground so that one day there will be more oak trees—and then more acorns. British to the beak, they declare by their act of

143

CARDINAL

forestry, that this country would be a sad place indeed if we were ever bereft of our hearts—and our trees—of oak.

This is what you see: A black necklace, a crest that rises or falls with the birds' passing moods, brilliant blue coat with black and white patches, a white vest and a blue train-length tail with white feather ruching at either side. Add a pair of roving black eyes and dancing feet, and you have a fairly complete picture of the northern blue jay.

Blue jays are silent only at nesting time. They're almost furtive then, for they don't want to draw the enemy's fire that might upset their plans for rearing more blue jays to plant more acorns. The male brings food to his mate so she won't have to go foraging for herself and leave the eggs to get chilled. He's a gallant gentleman, attentive to his lady's every wish. And he never calls her wishes whims! The two are dressed as much alike as twins, and it would require a museum curator to tell them apart.

Blue jays build with care. First they construct

144

a durable framework from select pieces of "timber" —often green twigs they have twisted off a tree. You seldom see them picking up any brittle sticks from the ground. Then they weave an inner lining of fine rootlets and grasses, with an occasional strand of horsehair when a pasture is conveniently near.

While many blue jays do winter in Canada, the majority probably fly away to some southern clime. Jean Brodie Firth sent us once an exciting news flash telling of hundreds of vivid blue wings seen sweeping through the rain towards the lake at a high point of the cliffs, out Scarboro way.

Mrs. Firth told how a hundred or more of these big blue birds with crests, had stopped to rest— and shake the rain from their tailed coats—in a tall pine tree on the height before crossing the great lake. And what a sight for a rainy day!

The cliff at that point is close to five hundred feet above Lake Ontario, and a logical place for migrating birds to cross. Not all our birds go south via Point Pelee.

Dr. W. W. H. Gunn's dictum re the migration of blue jays confirms this account. The executive director of the Federation of Ontario Naturalists is a high avian authority and we are glad to quote him:

It is true that we have blue jays here in Ontario all the year around, but it is an open question whether the ones we see in our gardens from season to season are always the same individuals.

Certainly, we know that great migrations of blue jays take place each spring and fall. In this locality the fall migration is the more obvious one.

145

He mentions that the many observers who were watching the hawk migration on September 20-21 could testify that hundreds and even thousands of blue jays were moving southwestward along the north shores of Lake Ontario and Lake Erie on those days and that this was "only a typical example of what may be seen on virtually any day during the latter part of September each year."

These birds apparently skirt the lakes and cross over into the central United States via Michigan and Ohio, Dr. Gunn further states. And he quotes a recent report from Mrs. Perry Reynolds of Detroit Audubon Society who had witnessed on September 28th "a very large migration of blue jays, approximately 15,000, travelling in loose, continuous flocks, through Essex County, toward the international border."

While vigorous young Canadians are skating, skiing, or just tramping across the country, hardy Northern Canada jays are going ahead with plans for their early nests made snug against February storms with a felting of squirrel or other fashionable fur, reinforced by dry moss, interwoven with feathers from passing fowls of the air that happen to shed them in jay territories.

The Canada jay is larger than a robin. The adult a dark grey with white throat, white forehead, and dark hood thrown on the back of his head. The juvenile has no light patches. Looks as though he had squeezed through a sooty chimney in his nice grey suit!

Let a hunter, trapper or bushman sit down beside his fire in the Northern Canadian woods in winter to eat his lunch, and he is almost sure to have several Canada jays visit him. They never seem at all afraid and will readily alight within a few feet of him to get a morsel of food—preferably meat.

One day an engineer on construction of the air base at Goose Bay, had an excellent chance to observe the behaviour of these companionable birds.

When the deer-hunter had "dressed his kill," the jays would work for days storing the fat (suet to you) they had filched from the animal's remains. Making no pretense to hide their plunder, the birds stowed it away in crotches of trees or other suitable places, where it would not likely be buried under snow, but available when wanted.

He noticed while in Labrador that Canada jays "seemed most numerous in black spruce muskeg where there was little if any bird or animal life," and he "often wondered what they fed on when nesting and living there." They start nest-building soon after the middle of March and select usually the lower limb of a spruce well exposed to the sun. He "presumed this was done in order to benefit from the heat rays reflected from the nearby snow."

Even after the eggs were laid, there were many days—and more nights—when the thermometer dipped well below zero. "And while some might think there was not much heat reflected from snow," the engineer described how he "actually gathered pussy willows in blossom when there was still four to five feet of snow under them." This was one first of April—and no joke!

Of Canada jay's nicknames, he could understand "meat bird," as appropriate, but he never quite saw the reason for "whiskey jack." The bird was anything but a roysterer. In fact, he was "almost Quakerish in appearance and manners, compared with the blue jay who was both loud in dress and vocally."

F. G. Speck, Indian lore authority, says all the Northern tribes call the Canada jay, wiskedjak (meat bird), the name altered by whites to whiskey jack. Hunters have found him not only a meat bird, but a soap bird. They say he runs off with bits of soap from the camp, and that he must eat them, as he has never been caught using them for washing. Matches and plugs of tobacco also disappear when wiskedjak calls. Another name is moose bird.

The Canada jay is one of the earliest of our northern birds to nest, sometimes as early as February 7th, at forty below. The nest of the Canada jay is a rare find so I was thrilled to have one sent to me by K. Gordon Miller from near Nestor Falls, fifty miles from Kenora. It was eleven inches in diameter and six inches deep, woven of twigs, strips of birch bark, catkins and dry moss. Inner cup lined with squirrel fur and partridge feathers. One egg was still in nest, pale grey with olive spots.

Dan McCowan, western naturalist, says the female Canada jay sits tight on nest, with snow all around her, to guard against a freeze of the eggs.

Her mate meanwhile brings her the bacon. It may be literally bacon, for that's how the bird got its name of "Camp Robber," since it will come boldly into camp and steal a rasher right off the pan.

I can find no record of a Canada jay ever having nested in Southern Ontario, though individuals have been seen here, now and again, during their winter wanderings. Curator L. L. Snyder saw one a few years ago back of the Summit Golf course near Aurora, Ontario. And Dr. R. M. Saunders reported one, the other winter, at the Eastern Gap, Fisherman's Island side.

Jean Brodie, journalist, tells us that when out west one summer she fed the Canada jays near Lake Louise, and on arriving home had one for a couple of days at their feeding station, out Scarboro way in Ontario, where she and her husband then lived.

Rather similar in colouring, but smaller is the loggerhead shrike who would be the farmers' friend if they'd let him. So would the northern shrike which is almost identical and occurs here as a winter visitor. Both have a swelled head and a hooked beak with which to destroy mice and grass-hoppers.

Shrikes could be called song birds of prey. They have a sharp hook and "tooth" at tip of beak with which to tear food—birds, lizards and such— which they catch by swift swoops like a hawk or in straight chase. And they can put up a gentle front by imitating part of the song of any small bird they want to attract. The name originated in bird's high pitched cry—a shriek.

149

Defenders of the shrike's habit of impaling victims on thorns (its other name is "butcher bird") claim the bird's feet are unfitted to grasp prey, so prospective food has to be hitched to something, and spiked bushes are handy. But when these are not available, shrikes have learned to make use of barbed wire—an effective substitute.

F. B. Rogers (St. Catharines) asked identification of an unfamiliar bird perched on a power wire seen from his window along Twelve-Mile Creek.

Mr. Rogers described the bird as about the size of a cardinal with a long tail, but with head and neck bulkier, and no crest. It flipped off the perch, he tells, dipped in flight, then wound up on another wire about twenty feet away. It soon dropped off that wire and "sort of sailed down to the bank of the creek and alighted behind a large timber out of my vision."

He could see weed stocks being shaken by the bird's activities. Then it came into view again and settled down with a small object in its claws which it struck at repeatedly with its beak and began tearing to pieces. Mr. Rogers took it to be a mouse or a mole, but wasn't close enough to be sure. My guess was a northern shrike. Male and female are dressed alike. The last time I saw a shrike was down in the Eastern Townships, Quebec, when driving from Dufferin Heights to Stanstead. Three of them were flying from tree to tree along the edge of a wood, and screaming. How funny! (I thought.) There go some black and white blue jays. For that is just what they looked like, until we drew near enough to note the large head, hooked beak and no crest.

Then I recognized the shrikes, having first seen them in my old county of Prince Edward. Head and back of the neck are grey, like a gull.

Of the two hundred kinds of shrikes four are found on this continent. They are not speedy fliers. Timed by motorists, they are grouped with hawks, herons and horned larks, as doing 22 to 28 miles an hour. Migratory flights of most birds occur in flock formation; shrikes are solitary travellers. When several are found together it is said to be an indication they have been "drawn by unusual conditions," such as abundant food.

Northern winters fail to terrify that valiant bit of fluff, the black-capped chickadee. His outer coat of feathers is deceptive. He looks delicate but is really rugged. Inside is a thick fleece lining and, under that, a tough skin stretched over layers of warm fat. That's where the suet you fed him went, in melted form, via an elastic throat. He has a central heating system set off by electric spark. It is said chickadee runs a temperature nine degrees higher than man.

A pair will chisel out a nest in pine or birch, picking a rotten stump for preference. It is fun to watch them flying off to a safe distance with the chiselled chips, to cover their tracks from enemy prowlers. They don't say (like the downie), "Hew to the line, let chips fall where they will!"

A short sharp beak drills the deep crevices for egg-clusters that would be canker worms—or worse

151

—come spring. Stout claws clamp into the bark, or weed stock, where he clings while husking seeds. Nothing seems to get the chickadee down except a sleet storm that coats the tree bark with frozen rain as hard as silver, so he can't get his teeth into the supply of insect calories. In summer he is a flycatcher of agility and seldom misses. He likes pumpkin seeds especially if cracked for him. Flocks separate in March and April and go pairing off to nest.

Besides his familiar gay song that named him, the chickadee has a two-tone phrase interpreted by some as "fee-bee!" Sounds to me like "spring's here!"

Emerson wrote of this gay little winter visitor as a "Scrap of valour who, just for play, fronts the north wind in waistcoat of grey." When chickadees come darting to our window sill on blustery days—in quick succession—cheerily calling their own name, between hammer blows on the sunflower seeds or broken walnuts, I am reminded of the rollicking "Nutcracker Suite."

Not much bigger than a chickadee is its cousin, the nuthatch, one of the most fascinating winter visitors. The white-breasted kind is dressed in slate-blue and white with black accents. Has been called a tree mouse, owing perhaps to its habit of travelling along the trunk in little staccato movements.

A friend, seeing a nuthatch the other day for the first time (in the big elm on our avenue), was quite excited. "Oh, see!" she said. "It runs around and 'round the tree just like a squirrel." The novice gets vivid first impressions.

One writer, of unquestioned ability to observe, says that in early spring the nuthatch "sings a pleasantly modulated, whistled song."

I have never heard a nuthatch produce anything but "Wah! wah! wah! wah! wah!" Sometimes repeated in accelerated tempo eight or nine times, on the same note and in a nasal tone. Some books say "Quank, quank," but the "k" is lost on me.

More than one reader, however, has assured me that the nuthatch really does go "musical" in spring. One of them quotes an English writer in praise of its "loud, clear ringing call."

"Little quank" is the pet name for the red-breasted nuthatch that summers as far north as Great Slave Lake. He holes-up in dead trees, preferably the white birch, and has a curious habit of making an artistic frame of pitch or balsam gum around his picture doorway.

It is a stubby-tailed bird an inch or so shorter than the white-breasted kind, and it has a black band through its eye widening into a plume-like tracery back to shoulder. Breast is more rusty than red specified in name. It calls "Ank! ank!" in a thin voice.

The nuthatch haunts the evergreen, and breeds from top of timberline in Canada, wherever the spruce tree grows, and down through the New England states to North Carolina. It's a down-head bird. No other tree-bird goes down the trunk head first. Nor does it brace its tail, like the woodpecker family, as an aid to clinging.

Roger Tory Peterson had an unusual experience with this bird during a trip with a Capt. Nickerson, in a small open boat to the fishing banks of Cape Cod, which he relates in one of his books. They had crossed Chatham Bars, "the choppy dangerous rips" that guarded the entrance to their moorings, and headed fifteen to twenty miles out where they cast anchor.

There were few birds, so they fished, Mr. Peterson tells, "the only birds of interest being, of all things, four red-breasted nuthatches! These came aboard one at a time, and crept mouselike over the ropes and woodwork. . . . These little waifs, at home only in the spruces and firs of the northwoods, were on one of their lemming-like journeys to destruction.

"They had probably flown on their stubby little wings all the way from Maine or Nova Scotia. When they left the boat they headed due south over the endless water—not landward toward the low line of dunes dimly visible on Monomoy to the west. They seemed so pitifully small as they started out for nowhere over the waves," Mr. Peterson concludes.

In a neglected garden one winter day I watched for half an hour four juncos going over the ground methodically. Heads bent, they hopped along, picking, picking, picking, and never seemed to miss an inch of seed infested territory.

When flitting to find fresh hunting patches,

each bird would show its conspicuous white banner of outer tail-feathers, the certain identification mark of the junco.

Not every bird lives up to its name like the junco (derived from the Latin juncus, a seed). It is called also black snowbird. Slate grey above, head and shoulders nearly black, its breast is pearl white. The short, effective seed-splitting beak is a pinky, straw colour.

Its slender legs look as if encased in skin-tight, black kid stockings. The young birds in summer are streaked, and might be confused with vesper sparrows which also have white tail-feathers. Though the vesper sparrow is brownish—not grey like the junco.

Slatey breeds as far north as Yukon, Newfoundland and Central Labrador, and winters wherever seeds are plentiful. It is not the cold he minds, so much as food shortage, and cereal is where he finds it.

Writing about the annual destruction of weed seeds by the junco (in the state of Iowa alone), F. E. L. Beal has recorded that on the basis of one-fourth of an ounce of seed eaten daily by each bird, and supposing that they remained in their winter range two hundred days, there would be a total of 1,750,000 pounds (or 875 tons) consumed by this one species in a single season. And Mr. Beal added that "large as these figures may seem, they certainly fall far short of the reality."

So unobtrusive a bird is not easily identified by the average observer. But a nuthatch spotted one the other day nibbling seeds on what he considered his exclusive dinner wagon. The nuthatch lowered his head and spread threatening wings, but the junco never budged. And the bluff, falling flat, the bluffer slipped quietly off the ledge.

Definitely winter birds, these slender little seed-eaters were constant callers at our window-ledge for the snowy months, but never an audible peep out of them. Warm weather seems to release some secret spring in their throats. For in mid-March while a patch of white frost—ghost of the late snow—still clung to a shaded corner of our brown garden, a slate junco flew to a leafless lilac and gave its salute to spring—the thin repeated chatter that sounds like the summer song of a chipping sparrow.

Always to me the most exciting of winter bird visitors is the cardinal. One came to us one New Year's Day—a gorgeous male in his red robes—to open the gate of the year, a splendid omen.

He hopped on the snowless ground of a vacant lot, behind the garden, stopping every few inches to pick at something in the stiff grass that seemed to his taste—weed seed probably. Most of the time he stayed in the shadow of near-by trees. But once or twice he stepped—deliberately it seemed—out into a band of sunlight.

Then the cardinal was splendid. Such a glowing red, like fluid—there was wine in his veins perhaps!

It is a matter of constant wonder that this essentially southern bird which once bred only in warm climes and among the richest and reddest of flowering vines in the privileged south has of its own free will—and free wing—come up here not only to nest in summer, but has stayed to winter in our so-called inhospitable north.

But the cardinal has the character and courage of good blood. He wanted adventure—to see more of the world. And, forsaking easy paths, came north prepared to adapt himself to the hard way. Some of our winters must have tested his courage a bit, when many of his kind cheerily picked their daily food of sunflower seeds from a three-feet-high table of snow.

In 1950 a flash from Mrs. D. W. MacKenzie of Victoria Harbour brought the news that redbirds had reached that territory. She was writing, it was explained, because we had asked her three years before if the cardinals had penetrated that far.

At the time cardinals were reported in Ottawa. I went out on a limb and predicted their ultimate limit as the North Pole, and that some fine day a brilliant red male might be seen perched on the top proclaiming territorial rights. Who knows?

Our cardinals have become the family alarm clock. Literally early birds, the first one comes to hammer on the window ledge at the crack of dawn, and no light sleeper could fail to hear the insistent blows of that firm red beak as he cracks the sunflower seeds. The clock is having a rest. The morning that it was "officially" five-below in downtown Toronto, the redbirds were at their post eating and singing.

There is a sharp contrast in winter and spring behaviour of Mr. Cardinal.

In the winter the male cardinal will drive the

157

lady away from the food tray. But in spring, when the young male's fancy lightly turns to thoughts of nesting, it is quite a different story.

The redbird at your window may be observed, any early spring day, gallantly picking up a sunflower seed, which he rolls in his beak to shed the shell, then tiptoes toward the grey lady and quite daintly (for a male) transfers the meaty kernel to her willing beak. Obvious bribery!

Why do cardinals go bumping and banging into window panes? Many queries have come this way from different parts of the country.

Mazo Park wrote from Mount Dennis, just up the hill from the Humber, that they had a cardinal the family calls "red the rivetter," who flew at all the windows and made a loud tapping with his beak. "And we seem to think it has something to do with the mating. As the season goes on he starts early in the morning and keeps it up till sundown."

The cardinals are, it is likely, fighting their own reflection in the glass. The bright male spots a rival rushing toward him in battle dress, his crest raised. The grey lady sees just another female cardinal who would be *de trop*, of course!

Cardinals remain most of the year near their nesting sites, though they may wander at intervals to explore other areas.

"Why were the cardinals singing so lustily now, when it was far from nesting time?" I asked Curator Snyder, for we have heard their merry whistle daily since January 24th. He said they "look for their territory early. . . . They have

probably selected their mates—as well as their
nesting sites—and they seem to like long engagements!"

A striking fellow is the great pileated woodpecker, with dazzling red conical crest, a white
bridle dangling down his slender neck—the neck
very powerful in spite of its slenderness—and an
overall black cloak with patches of silver lining.
He is unchallenged cock of our deep northern woods
and a truly wild bird.

The cock-of-the-woods has four powerful toes
on each foot, two fore and two aft, and these with
the aid of ten tail-spikes, give him a firm stance on
the tree while he hunts grubs and fat insects. A
pair may take a month to complete their deep
dugout in some skyscraping pine or other fir tree,
often seventy or eighty feet above ground, the two

working in shifts at the nest. So many big chips fly out from the operation, that the 'peckers could hang out a sign, "Axemen at Work," and be believed.

The long stout beak is like a wedge with which it splits the bark—both for excavating the nest cavity, and grubbing for destructive pests. The tip of its tongue has a spearpoint hard as bone, and near the tip is a file of bristles reversed, so that when this instrument is pried into a worm-filled crevice, the worm may turn—but it cannot escape!

The name is derived from "pileus" a cap, "a brimless, round felt cap worn by ancient fishermen and sailors" and "by all the people" during a Saturnalia—the annual festival formerly held at Rome.

Milord and lady are both red-crested, and go shouting and tap-tapping through the wild northern timbers in a truly festal way. A slight difference in the pair is that the male has the rouge cheeks.

Next to the vanishing ivory-billed woodpecker whose twenty-inch ghost may still haunt the southern cypress swamps, the pileated wood-pecker—to give it its bookish name—is the largest woodpecker on this continent.

J. B. May says that the ivory-bill's "disappearance" cannot be blamed entirely on the "more civilized white man," and he quotes Mark Catesby (who published a natural history in 1731) that the "bills of these birds were much valued by the Canada Indians who made coronets of 'em for their princes and great warriors, by fixing them around a wreath with their points outward. The Northern

Indians (Catesby noted), having none of these birds in their cold country, purchase them from the southern people, at the price of two, and sometimes three, buckskins a bill."

To return to our own (luckily not vanishing) species. The pileated woodpecker is known to be highly beneficial. It not only confines its activities to dead wood, but where it rips off the bark it consumes enormous schools of insects. And when it wants to draw in one of these frequent feasts of succulent slugs this pecker can stick out its long, barbed and gluey tongue farther than the average schoolboy, and well beyond the tips of its horny mandibles.

All good foresters, when they hear his resounding call through the deep woods, are glad. And they do not complain of the untidy heaps of chips on the ground.

A young hunter, new to the game, might covet one of these handsome birds, to boast about at home. But he'd better watch out for the warden on his trail! The Migratory Birds Convention Act prohibits the shooting of any woodpecker—any time. In fact the hunting of insect-eating birds is entirely forbidden.

The downy, a most engaging winter bird and our smallest woodpecker, is very tiny beside the crow-size pileated woodpecker. By day, downy may visit your suet station to fill his food tank. But during the long winter nights he will snuggle down in some warm tree-hole until March, when he hunts a mate.

The hairy woodpecker is a big brother of the

161

downy. The only material difference is in size. Both have a wide white stripe down the back, and curved bands of ermine from base of beak to back of head. On the head of the male, the upper band is fastened with a bright red chevron.

On a sunny March day, the hairy woodpecker is likely to begin his tattoo on the most resounding tree he can find, as a signal that he is ready to discuss housekeeping. If any lady likes the music of it, she may fly to meet him half way, and together they will select the site and chisel out a knothole to shelter the future family of three, four or five young woodpeckers.

Down South some folks call the smaller varieties, "peckwoods." In Southeastern Georgia, in the gloom of the swamplands, but with the scent of yellow jasmine to cheer him, the naturalist is ever on an insatiable hunt for the swiftly vanishing ivory-billed woodpecker. This giant of the species—also most beautiful and the wildest—is to be sought only after tedious tramping through dense brakes of cane and bay-bushes to reach the stands of cypress and live-oak, and at the end—a jungle of great pines where a few untameable ivory-bills may still be found.

All the "peckwoods" have large sturdy heads and slim strong necks. Our common hammer was doubtless patterned after the woodpecker's natural tool. I once watched a hairy woodpecker at Centre Island brace himself by his tail spikes and hammer off pieces of bark, half as big as himself, from the trunk of a willow tree. His nostrils are protected by stout hairy tufts—hence his name.

SCREECH OWL

Owls are said to be a race by themselves. Their link with other species has long puzzled ornithologists. They just don't seem to have any near relations. They have large eyes encircled by a curious disc of radiating feathers. They generally take their prey—not by pursuit but by surprise— their soft feathers ensuring a noiseless approach.

They are birds of the night, and in old English books you will find the term "by owl-light," used to indicate dusk or twilight. Because of its chiefly night life, when its activities cannot readily be observed by humans, the owl has always been festooned with fables. Among the Kootenay Indians, there was the legend of the wicked owl that had the habit of flying off with children. It was killed at last by an avenger and its body burned; but its (unburnt) spirit rose from the ashes in a more unpleasant form: The owl became a swarm of blood-thirsty mosquitoes.

In Puerto Rico a visiting naturalist was warned there were native owls that would steal the hats right off the heads of men who "walked the trails" at night, and carried them off to make nests in. Pima Indians believed that at death the human soul passed into the body of an owl. So, to assist in the transmigration, they would collect a complete outfit of owl feathers and place them in the hands of a dying person.

Owls figure frequently in Shakespeare, where more than six hundred references to birds have been noted. There are three hundred kinds of owls known, from the tiny elf, to the great horned owl which often measures two feet from crown to tail-tip. The great horned owl is the earliest bird to nest in the Toronto area. A dauntless bird watcher discovered one of these owls nesting high up in a swaying pine tree, on February 13, 1943. And if you remember what a bitter month that February was, you will know the sitting bird must have held its body close to the Plimsoll line in order to keep the two or three snowy eggs from freezing. The pair take turns in incubating the eggs, which require twenty-eight days to hatch—and about forty days more before the youngsters can go mousing for themselves.

The ear tufts of the great horned owl are mere blinds. His real ears are concealed under feather cones that serve as ear trumpets. He has a lid to his ear that he can open or close at will. So when he doesn't want to hear unpleasant news—or some farmer swearing at him for chiselling his chickens— well, the owl has the remedy in his own head—just pulls down his ear flaps.

Owls live chiefly on fresh-killed animals which they capture and eat. This species will even dine on baby skunks; though, if in fastidious mood, may devour only the brains of its prey.

A great horned owl once killed during the season fifty guinea-fowl; picked their brains and left the flesh untouched. Or so it was recorded. And a Rosebank observer declares that some anaemic bird of prey in his area makes incisions in the side of hen after hen (deft as a surgeon) and extracts their livers.

At Toronto Island eleven of these great owls were shot in one year, the park chief told me. One was caught in a willow tree with an enormous rabbit in its claws.

The great horned owl is not only a great hunter, but an expert fisherman. But because his activities occur after dark—not in broad daylight like the fish hawk—he has had a small gallery of watchers to record his methods of operation.

A keen bird watcher just back from his cottage on Lonely Lake (Sault Ste. Marie) had fun watching one of these big owls at work catching fish without line or jack-light. "There was not even a moon," he reported. "But the spectacular pantomime was clearly visible, from our veranda, against the afterglow in the west reflected on the surface of the lake, after dusk, as in a mirror."

As he described it, the owl would perch on a fallen log beside the mouth of a small creek that emptied into the lake, apparently watching for stray fish coming down stream. Then he would spread his broad wings, silently lift himself into the air and alight on a branch of an overhanging tree, to be used as a springboard.

The show, in sharp silhouette, was exciting. Observing the surface being broken by the leaping of silvery fish, the owl with accurate timing (and spacing) would swoop down from his perch and grab one—merely getting his feet wet in the process—and away he would go to the log with his fish supper, which he would devour—scales and all probably.

And fish are not the only prey the great horned owl retrieves from the lakes and rivers at night. Forbush states that they pick both wild and domestic ducks out of the water, "and no goose is too large for them to tackle." But as the great horned owl is very destructive to rats, he should be excused if he nabs a goose or two.

A very large snowbird is the dazzling white owl from the Canadian Arctic called the snowy owl. It's as big as a great horned owl, but minus the hoot-owl's horns, giving snowy's head an absurdly flat look, like a skullcap or modern beanie.

The males are very white; the females are larger than males and have dusky spots; juveniles are mottled. The legs are sheathed in feathers to toes. Even the owl's deadly bill is masked in fluff.

They nest on the ground, across Polar territory at the top of both worlds—from Northern Russia to Greenland, to our Arctic and Alaska. They fly fearlessly across the ocean, and have been known to alight on ships a thousand miles from land.

The largest snowy owl drift on record occurred in 1926, when hundreds of these live feathered parachutes showered down over Southern Ontario. I happened to be in Niagara-on-the-Lake at the time and there saw my first snowy owl outside of picture books.

One had been captured and placed for safe keeping in a chicken house (the chickens having been removed first, of course), and half the towns-people came to look. The owl's topaz eyes seemed to blaze with fury at the indignity of being cooped up in such a place, though it was better than being shot as so many of his tribe were that year. That was sheer slaughter.

How much better to shoot one of these beautiful visitors from the Arctic—with a camera—than to blow it to bits with powder and shot. Not to mention the rule of hospitality shattered when these refugees from a lemming-less tundra, who come to our fields for food, are given the gun instead.

Every few years (some authorities say four, others eight or ten) the snowies come down from the Arctic to hunt a living here—mostly field mice. They may pluck the odd rabbit, but that would help save the farmers' fruit trees. They come here, it is generally agreed, because of a shortage of

167

lemmings on the northern tundra, and queries have come as to the nature of these little "beasties" and why the periodic shortage.

According to Charles Elton, a British authority, the lemming is a mouse-like rodent, the largest member of the family of Arctic mice. It is described as "a diamond edition of the guinea-pig," with plump body, short stumpy tail, a Roman nose, and "swift gait that denies the apparent intention of its body." It has a coat of grey fur with dark stripe down its back—the coat turning whitish in winter.

Nocturnal in habit, lemmings live under the snow in winter. Eat roots as well as plants on the tundra, liquorice root being a favourite item which they cache in their runways. Eskimo women are said to rifle their caches for the succulent roots with which to flavour their fish and meat cakes.

But the robbing of their food hoards is not set down by Mr. Elton as cause of the lemmings' periodic migrations which, in turn, drive the snowies down to Ontario and other points south.

He thinks it may be due to "cyclical over-abundance" of mouse population, together with the decimating by predators, and disease caused by overcrowding. He cites the migration of the snowies, after the lemming debacle, as "one of the most remarkable features of the Arctic cycle," and says "it affects the equilibrium of animal population thousands of miles south of the tundra."

Mr. Elton notes the "predominant importance" of lemmings for the snowy owl, calling these mice its "anchor" in the Arctic, and states that when they are gone the snowy "drifts away, seeking other means of subsistence."

He relates the classic fable (from Robert Bridges) of how the lemmings in Norway, when their offspring increased, "bravely forsook their crowded nests in the snow" and swarmed over the plains to ravage field and farm; and "in unswerving course ate their way to the coast, where, plunging down the rocks, they swam in the salt sea to drowning death."

Winter is the wandering season when owl tribes become restless, like the early Redskins, and go roving from place to place for better hunting. Among nomads coming down from their northern range in the Arctic, or from Ungava, or Greenland, are the short-eared owls who, like the snowy, may often be seen flying in daytime, especially when it is overcast or foggy, though they prefer twilight or moonshine.

And all this species asks is open country— meadow or marshland, with hedgerows or tall grass at hand for quick hideouts—and lots of mice.

Short tufts, like sprouting horns, rise out of the owl's head. Though tufts are short, the ear proper is cavernous.

The owl's eyes are bright yellow, but the pupil is so big and black the gold is hidden. It looks straight at you with both eyes at once, not like birds that regard you coyly with only one eye at a time. Feet are feathered to the toe-nails which have an elegant shine. Their flight as fluffy as a night moth. The owl appears to float on the air.

If annoyed, the bird can hiss like escaping

steam and snap his mandibles. When startled by an invader of his territory, he will rise and fly, and, like Lot's wife, looks back over his shoulder to see what's coming. What's coming may not be salt, but a charge of shot. Which is a pity, since short-ears' food is mostly rodent. Six mice have been found in one owl's interior.

Owls have been known to come down Toronto chimneys, bringing puffs of sticky black soot in their wings. These chiefly nocturnal birds need sharp ears as well as eyes in order to detect their prey. The long-eared species is a bird of the "murmuring pines and the hemlocks." The showy top tufts are not ears really—merely feather horns. The things they hear with are large apertures that occupy the whole side of head behind the eyes and covered by liftable flaps of skin which the owl can raise or lower at will. Compared with the ears of day birds, those of owls are elephantine though (unlike the elephant) they do not flap where you can see them but are concealed under a drape of feathers.

Besides being a genuine Canadian, longears is the common owl of Ireland and its directional finding apparatus is most effective. Stuart Smith (in the Leader) calls it "master of the silent pounce" with ears that can hear the nibbling of a mouse.

The eyes are the most fascinating feature which Mr. Smith cleverly dubs "natural windscreen wipers." They have a membranous third eyelid that flicks back and forth over the owl's eyeball to clean and lubricate its organ of vision.

Chiefly because it is nocturnal, and very small, the saw-whet owl is not well known. But it is definitely worth knowing, for it is very beautiful, arrayed in finely patterned plumage of rich brown, creamy white, and with patches of yellow feathers to match its topaz eyes. To me it's the most exquisite little thing in feathers, about the size of a folded hand, with yellow feathered feet, and unbelievably gentle.

Because they are birds of the night, mostly desecrating the darkness with weird cries, the whole family of mousing owls has been given a bad name by Shakespeare and others—and the name has stuck. An old Greek legend gives the "infernal regions" as the owl's place of origin, though it was Minerva's favourite bird.

French folklore has put an odd twist in the owl character: One day a wren flew into the sky to fetch down a few shafts of fire to warm other birds that had the shivers, but the little benefactor got its own feathers singed while doing its good deed for the day. To show their gratitude each of the others gave the wren a feather from their own coat to replace that which he had lost.

The owl alone refused, and on the ground that he would need all his feathers for the coming winter. This caused him to be shunned by those who thought themselves more virtuous, and was given as reason for the owl, and his descendants, keeping out of sight all day.

When asked by readers intrigued with these stories of birds, how to go about getting to know them, we generally suggest winter as the best time of year to start bird study. First, there are not nearly so many around to confuse the beginner, and not nearly so many leaves to obscure the view. Get a note-pad and a few pencils and go out!

To the many who ask how best to attract the birds, a concise answer was given by Alexander Sprunt, who said that all essentials necessary to a bird's existence were "an abundance of food, water and cover." A sinister suggestion is contained in the word "cover." Safety from predators such as cats. It is not severe cold that causes them to perish (because their blood temperature is ten degrees higher than man's) but lack of food, the books say. And they can't dig down under the snow, like a squirrel, when hungry.

It would help if every owner of a tree or clothes-line would hang out bags of nuts and hunks of suet in winter, not only to provide food for the birds but fun for the bird watchers! And for drink, birds can sip snow.

My sister, who was a lover of birds (as well as gardens) and had always been an inspiration to me in my work, had marked this passage written by Joseph Addison:

There is another circumstance in which I am very particular or, as my neighbours call me, very whimsical; as my garden invites into it all the birds of the country, by offering them the conveniency of springs and shades, solitude and shelter.

I do not suffer anyone to destroy their nests in the spring or drive them from their usual haunts in fruit-time. I value my garden more for being full of blackbirds, than cherries, and very frankly give them fruit for their songs.